C000000737

Nimblicity™

From
Aristotle
to Zuckerberg:
Communication
Wisdom that **Wins**

NICHOLAS WRIGHT
AND DARREN BRIGGS

Nimblicity

First published in 2022 by

Panoma Press Ltd
a Rethink Press company
www.rethinkpress.com
www.panomapress.com

The authors will donate 10% of their royalties to The University of Sydney Indigenous Student scholarships.

Book layout by Neil Coe.

978-1-784529-63-5

Nimblicity is a trademark of Borealis AG. The term and trademark "Nimblicity" was created by Borealis and represents one of Borealis' core values. The term stands for: We are fit, fast and flexible and seek smart and simple solutions. We encourage decisions on all levels of the organisation to increase ownership and speed to realisation. We welcome change and manage it to shape our future. The authors would like to thank Borealis for their kind permission to use Nimblicity in this book.

CONTENTS

INTRODUCTION

We are not the kind of people who would write this kind of book.

For a start, the pair of us are drop-outs. One expelled from school, the other flunked every exam he ever attempted. But strangely, we have found ourselves on parallel journeys in the worlds of business and politics, influencing people – in a positive way – through the way we communicate. Initially by accident, perhaps, but later in life… certainly with intention.

The corporate one

For the one who underachieved at school and flunked his exams, the first insight into the persuasive power of communication was in an entry-level job at British Airways and their Cargo Division. With a handful of bad grades to his name, his perception was that of a torrent of graduates passing him by, all armed with degrees, hubris and high-flying careers to match. Meanwhile, he was marooned, left flightless on the runway. This feeling was only reinforced when informed by a union rep that most people at BA Cargo performed the same job for three decades or more, and only the lucky ones managed to escape and find a new job in a more glamorous part of the airline. The realisation gradually dawned that he had to do something about it or end up like lost luggage stuck in a cargo container. And so, courses were researched, expletives uttered, and careful consideration was given as to how much help the 'world's favourite airline' might offer.

He arranged a meeting with Mr Procter, the most senior manager in the department. It was all very formal and hierarchical in those days, and getting time with someone a good five or six levels higher (basically a lifetime in career terms) was akin to getting an audience with the Pope. He required an eye-catching reason. The door was opened when he asked if he could have ten minutes to share an idea to improve staff morale – a shrewd approach, given that employee relations were at a pretty low ebb at the time.

So, with his foot firmly jammed in the door, he made his case about how great it would be for BA to sponsor him to study at college to earn his Business Studies diploma. It would 'send a signal' to the entire department – of some 800 people or more – that he and the business were supportive of developing employees and that this would be good for morale.

Having reached first base and with the chutzpah of youth coursing through his veins, he then made an even bigger ask. He needed a paid day off each week for two years to attend the college. That would be unprecedented for British Airways, so Procter said that he would need some time to think about it, but the following day said yes with a smile.

That was back in 1986, the heyday of Maradona and Margaret Thatcher. He completed his diploma successfully, and as a result, Procter asked him to get involved in a major communications project – a first opportunity to break out of the 'job for life' that would otherwise probably have been his fate. It included a first taste of professional communications and involved presenting in front of 1,500 British Airways 'lifers' in the cargo warehouse. Not the easiest or friendliest of environments; the place was probably better thought of as a unionised bear pit for this young and ambitious greenhorn.

Despite various prophets of doom predicting that he would be stuck in his cargo role for three decades or more, he continued his educational journey by gaining an MBA from Lancaster University Management School in 1995 and then moved into a variety of – progressively more responsible, senior and rewarding – roles at British Airways, Microsoft, Nike, PepsiCo and Vodafone.

After a short spell with The Company Agency in 2008, Darren formed his own business that has worked with leaders and organisations in over 30 countries, helping them perform and change better through effective internal communication.

The thing to remember is that *none* of this would have happened without a keen (and largely self-taught) ability to communicate with influence. To get his employer to *do* something that it seldom had – if ever – done before. To get other people's perceptions to change or improve in a positive way and them to think, feel and do things differently. Just as important was the *emotive* drive, in part to prove people wrong to write him off after such a humble academic start.

Not least among these was himself.

The political one

The other author – having *excelled* – found himself unceremoniously (and somewhat unjustly) *expelled*, having displeased a prickly principal through his editorship of the school magazine. His teenage rebellion came in the form of satire, but his headteacher expected a *Pravda*-like exercise, singing out his school's soaring accomplishments. Perhaps a career in progressive political campaigning was the inevitable result. Expulsion at the crucial age of 17 could have proven to be disastrous, but – through being taught the value of humility and made to start at the bottom, working nights at a factory – it turned out to be the making of him.

After stints travelling in Australia, France and a period as a lifeguard in the United States, he found himself volunteering at his local MP's office, who introduced him to the Palace of Westminster. That turned into a placement at Party HQ in the run-up to the 2001 general election (perhaps best remembered for the sitting deputy prime minister punching a voter in the face). He later found out that his chair in 'Rapid Rebuttal' would subsequently be occupied by none other than one Jacinda Ardern. Having become hooked to the smoke and gunfire of campaigns since the ludicrous age of 13 – running his best buddy's bid to be student president – he never missed an opportunity to get stuck in. Even if that meant leafleting for his 'eccentric' local MP, Jeremy Corbyn. All the while he continued to rebuild his academic education, picking up his BA and eventually an MSc in Global Politics and Economics from the Universities of Sheffield and London.

He earned his crust at the International Crisis Group NGO and then a couple of private-sector jobs – including meeting his co-author at the London management consultancy, The Company Agency (TCA). Nick finally found himself working for the legendary Washington wordsmith and linguist, Dr Frank Luntz. That led to experience leading campaigns across the Americas as well as some 25 other countries, everywhere from Sweden to Pakistan. Throughout, the lessons of what *won* – as well as those that did not – were burned into memory. Again, that desire and *need* to learn… as well as to prove the sceptical voices (internal and external) wrong, was vital fuel for the fire.

Eventually, he founded his own firm in Australia, working for those campaigns and causes he believed in – whether End of Life Choice (euthanasia) in New Zealand or girls' education in Pakistan. Sentio continues to thrive on three continents today, with clients ranging from Amnesty International to Airbnb. At the company's heart is a belief in continual *listening* and learning what is going on around you in order to effect real change. High-quality research and rational, well-reasoned advice. Nick still works as the CEO, as well as being co-owner of the social media polling start up Stickybeak. He can also be found teaching graduate students at Sydney and NYU Abu Dhabi campuses. It is all a long way from a shy, terrified teen making prawn mayonnaise in the ice cold of the night shift.

Reasons to read on...

We first started talking about this book one evening in Washington DC. One had been helping the World Bank develop its strategy to engage internal and external stakeholders; the other was working with the Bipartisan Policy Commission on vital immigration reform in the United States. Having worked together at TCA a decade before, we had stayed in touch as friends. Among the projects we shared then were helping HSBC better engage with its workforce, employee engagement for one of the world's largest hotel chains and London's winning bid for the 2012 Olympics.

What struck us now was the rapid pace of change brought on by technology, as well as how so many laws of good communication remained essentially *un*changed throughout this revolution. This applied, whether you were trying to get a voter to put a cross in a box or get an employee to promote a brand. And through chatting about our kids' effortless expertise with new media, it struck us that there were useful lessons for *anyone* seeking to improve their communications skills in the age of TikTok.

For instance, we both found ourselves frequently approached by quite senior figures – whether CEO or senator – who wanted to do something smart through social media or 'big data'. And often, this would be without having given much thought to *what* they were ultimately trying to achieve; *why* was the digital avenue appropriate in the first place? They just knew that it was important.

At the same time, we noted a paradox happening all around us. The world of data, analytics and technology promotes a view of the world that is based upon reason and rationality. But people remain people – incredibly *emotive*, irrational creatures, who spend far more of our lives behaving unconsciously than we would like to admit.

We don't pretend that this was a devastatingly new insight, but it did lie behind so many of the cockups and calamities that we had borne witness to throughout our careers. These stories are always more fun to listen to than your latest triumph, and by the end of the evening, we realised that we had a whole *trove* of them. At the time, Donald Trump was in the White House, Theresa May was triggering Article 50 (confirming Britain's exit from the EU) and Harvey Weinstein was heading for prison. All of this seemed to confirm the 'New Power' of online mass movements. And then, we were confronted by a once-in-a-century pandemic and a US election that dramatically reversed the Trump tidal wave of just four years before.

Did this negate the tools and techniques that had served Trump's victory so well in the first place? How have the revolutions of 'Web 5.0' and COVID-19 evolved the communications environment? And what are some of the lessons that have survived through all the upheaval of recent years and decades? This book seeks to provide at least some of the answers.

There are a lot of misconceptions about the role of the campaign manager or communications consultant. Ultimately, this is not a 'self-help' business book with models or ten-step plans for readers to follow slavishly. Instead, our intent is to share some stories to illuminate the most important communication lessons we have learned from working with leaders of every kind. As we shall see, we are all story telling creatures at heart.

Nor is it a book for commentators or critics, as it doesn't follow any one ideology or set of ideas as the route to Utopia. We are *empiricists*, more interested in showing some examples of what we have found actually *works* rather than trying to blind you with the brilliance of our theories.

Our starting point is the belief that in order to truly change the world, first, you must *understand* it. So if you are interested in *how* to effect positive, meaningful change and engage with the world on a deeper level – even as the means of communication change all around us – then this book is for you.

How the book is organised...

The world has always been – like people themselves – chaotic and maddening in spite of whatever rules and reason we try to impose on it. We *think* we understand ourselves, but we do not. We believe that we have free will and are utterly unpredictable when neither of these things is true. And yet, we still treat communication as if 'what I said' is the same thing as '*what was understood*'. What has changed in recent years is the *speed* and *strength* of the tides we are trying to manage, and we need a new approach to navigate these more effectively.

The advent of new communications technology has foisted new norms upon us all. Listening is now more important than the art of '*making friends and influencing people*'. After all, almost anyone can be an influencer. An introverted teenager – even if the daughter of Swedish celebrities – can have more impact on the conversation about climate change than a rock star. We are, all of us, becoming more sophisticated in how we communicate, as the gap between leader and follower gets smaller all the time. Nevertheless, there is part of us – all of us – that remains more chimp-like than we would ever like to admit, whether that is our need to belong to a 'tribe' or in the allure of an alpha figure in a power suit and red tie.

CEOs can (and mostly feel they *must*) talk directly with employees, bypassing layers of management. Reams of data from neuroscientists and psychologists tell them how to proceed. But that genie is out of the bottle. People don't want to engage with intermediaries, even as they are acutely aware of being 'spun' or 'sold out' by a system too complex to grasp and too large to be under control. Yes, the world is moving faster, becoming ever noisier. But paradoxically, this demands that you take *extra* time to get it right. To inculcate these lessons *faster*. And here, the circle loops back to the start.

Many of the tripwires that catch us out are, in fact, as ancient as the written word itself. The Roman emperor and stoic philosopher Marcus Aurelius has his place every bit as much as Alexandria Ocasio-Cortez, the youngest woman to ever serve in the United States Congress... Winston Churchill can still teach us as much as the latest anthropological 'big data' set. More senior leaders than you would think fall prey to the simple 'truisms' you might read in a newspaper column. They still talk about *themselves* rather than putting their *audience* in the picture. They hide in jargon rather than run the risk of plain speaking. Or simply speak more than they listen. This book sets out both the most common mistakes we *all* make from time to time and explains how and why the world of communication is transforming – and, we believe, for the better..

While this is emphatically *not* a 'self-help' book, our goal is to share our experience with people who currently, and aspire to, lead. We want to use our experience to show what they *should* be thinking about doing to influence others in a world that is getting 'noisier' every day. Rather than loading you with academic theory and concepts, our approach is based on sharing real-life stories and offering pragmatic and practical lessons.

And from this experience, we have identified ten important principles or 'laws' that every leader must take heed of when it comes to the way they communicate. Collectively, we have called them 'The Art of Nimblicity', and each chapter dives into each of the Nimblicity laws and how they can be applied. Using stories and real-life examples, they shine new light through old windows when it comes to the important considerations that any leader needs to contemplate when seeking to win others over to their cause or campaign.

The golden thread

Many people have asked us what key insights we have gained from writing this book, or simply, "what's the golden thread?"

The simple truth is that effective communication is a frustrating mix of both art and science. Just as you think you've established a solid working *heuristic* (or rule of the road), somebody comes along as an exception to that rule. However, there are recurring patterns that differentiate the communication efforts of the successful from those that fall flat.

The first is that communication isn't a linear, logical process where if I do 'X', then 'Y' will happen. Human psychology creates unpredictability in an audience that can't be... well, predicted. We want our communication *personalised* and to be treated as an individual, even as we form part of the crowd. The ability to project oneself as an authentic, empathetic human being – whether in Richard Branson's carefully cultivated 'rogue billionaire' image or FDR's cosy 'fireside chats' – is one of the most enduring communications challenges for those who lead.

As with any difficult challenge, it's essential to have a playbook that guides you to a successful outcome. Our playbook is called ORACLE and effectively forms six tests that every leader should consider before opening their mouth or hitting the 'send' button. We'll talk more about this in our opening chapter.

It is not just about being a brilliant public speaker anymore. Today's most influential communicators have to master the art of 'EQ' emotional intelligence – with the IQ of the online world. From the latest digital tools to metaphor and messaging, smart leaders know how to leverage both the art and science of communication to their advantage.

And finally, the big one. As our world grows more complex, connected and congested by the day with information overload, from the message to the channel of communication, the 'secret sauce' of success is *simplicity*.

Let's get started.

LAW OF NIMBLICITY #1:

PAY CLOSE ATTENTION TO WHAT IS HAPPENING AROUND YOU

"Attention is living; inattention is dying. The attentive never stop. The inattentive are dead already."

Buddha

Twenty-first-century technology hasn't just changed how we communicate; it has fundamentally altered human *consciousness*. Using a 20th-century formula is a recipe for failure. Successful communication is built on being able to 'pivot' on the mood of the moment. This requires successful leaders having a new mindset and reprogramming the way they communicate. It's time to think differently.

The approach that we have created is called '**Nimblicity**' – built around being NIMBLE, which has its roots in the Old English word 'nemel', which means quick to grasp (quick, agile, adaptable), and SIMPLICITY from the Latin word 'Simplicitas', which means a 'state of being simple, clarity, candour and directness'.

Why? The advancement of information technology has brought three factors to the fore, as never before: firstly, **speed** and **agility** – what used to happen in weeks or days now takes minutes or even *seconds*. But this isn't just a question of speed; the successful require a quickness of thought and adaptability if they are to avoid becoming roadkill. As an audience, we have become accustomed to demanding a response as rapid as a delivery from Uber Eats.

The second is the **democratisation** of communication. Power has become more diffuse. The immediacy of information demands that we communicate with a simplicity and a clarity that was not necessary or even desirable before. In a world where everybody can communicate directly with everyone else... you always need an answer ready.

Thirdly, we have never been more **interconnected**. Our governments can seem as helpless as they are hapless in the face of challenges that respect no national borders. Whether climate change or COVID-19... terrorism or tax evasion, increasingly we can only solve the world's problems if we are prepared to co-operate. Every campaign is a coalition of interests and individuals, so an approach that is as nimble as it is clear and simple is the only way to succeed.

Emotions are the currency of change

Leaders are drowning in data. Whether the boardroom chairwoman... the businessman... Premier League football coach or the most committed social activist, *all* depend on a multitude of facts and figures right at their fingertips. But facts *all* come with points of view. And successful communication is determined by understanding the other part of our brain: the emotional, ungovernable side. Our passions, fears and foibles are the drivers of social change, no matter your tribe or organisation… whether you seek to sell more goods or score more goals.

We can all think of recent instances when the 'rational' result simply didn't occur. Perhaps the dollar and data-driven Democrat campaign in the 2016 presidential election, defeated by the astounding surge of Donald Trump (and after that, his graceless defeat). The Brexit shock. Or the Tunisian fruit-seller Mohamed Bouazizi, whose sheer frustration at the bureaucratic bullying of totalitarianism caused him to self-immolate and thus spark the Arab Spring. What is at play when these – seemingly increasingly common – 'freak results' occur amid a wellspring of mass emotion?

As researchers, it is the emotional *underpinnings* of people's opinions that should most interest us – not simply what they report on the surface. But our emotional make-up remains shrouded in mystery and misinformation. We still have a decidedly *irrational* fear of wanting to discuss and dissect our 'feelings'. Many otherwise very intelligent people lack the vocabulary to go much beyond what makes us 'happy' or 'angry'. We witness a death and still think it 'unmanly' to cry. If we describe somebody as behaving 'emotionally' in any situation, it is not considered to be complimentary. It is as though to act on one's feelings is to somehow have failed as a human being. And yet, if you fail to grasp an astute understanding of the lexicon of emotion, you can never expect to communicate, lead or campaign effectively.

So, the first part of this chapter looks at how emotion – and collective mood – drives change. Then we discuss some of the ways you can better understand what is driving the sentiment of your audience. Human beings have always been aware of factors such as status and autonomy, fairness and certainty, each of which has undergone profound change in recent years. So we'll explore how we got here before looking at what is likely to come next. Throughout, we'll show some examples of how the smartest change-makers, CEOs and communicators demonstrate a new way of getting their message across.

Matching your MOOD to the moment...

For thousands of years, the wisest leaders and communicators have understood that the *emotional* connection has always been more important than the *rational*. It was Greek trickster (and god of fire) Prometheus who first said that "those whom the Gods wish to destroy, first they drive mad." When our blood is up – whether driving or dating – we seldom make sensible decisions. But how often are we *truly* aware of the sentiments that motivate us? Think of the stories you tell *yourself* – about your upbringing or those who have done you wrong... how often do they stand up to the real rigour of rational, impartial analysis?

It is our feelings that govern who we follow. In mass communication, the vital tool of political leaders, our feelings, hopes and fears were first addressed through the *written* word – whether through a bible or newspaper. Then radio allowed the huddled masses to *hear* our leaders. Next, television gave us a visual means through which to interpret them. Now, the plethora of peer-to-peer social media channels has given us an unprecedented means of gauging how our leaders, bosses and icons feel.

It is striking how our feelings combine as a group – whether a crowd, company or country – to create a *climate* as changeable as the weather overhead. Remember that Donald Trump's surprise 2016 victory was not his first attempt. His campaign in 2000 ended prematurely and pathetically. It took four more cycles for his message of insurgency at incumbent incompetence (... or, if you prefer, division, discord and thinly disguised bigotry) to strike a chord with the climate of the times. And then only four years for him to seem completely *dissonant* with them. It wasn't COVID-19 that saw him lose after only a single term. It was his reaction to COVID-19.

Fast-forward to two years later. The insurgent victory of a 28-year-old Alexandria Ocasio-Cortez over her establishment Democrat opponent in New York had more in common with Trump's own than either of them would like to acknowledge. Both put their 'outsider' status at the heart of their appeal. Both were outspent by massive margins (usually the most common predictor of success in US elections). And to both, it just didn't matter. They *mirrored the mood* of their voter audience to an almost astonishing degree.

This explains the importance of getting the *emotional context* right. Articulation of context – the 'where we find ourselves today' part of your story – should form *at least* half of your communication. Policy – what we tend to think elections are all about – by contrast, is actually the *smallest* component. Twenty per cent or less of a good piece of communication. The remaining third or so should focus on the future – where you want to take people and an appeal to their hopes. In the end, if you cannot show that you 'get' how they really feel and what they really want, your story will fail.

The ORACLE test

The word ORACLE comes from the Latin verb ōrāre, 'to speak' (think 'oral' and 'orate'). Given its historical connection to communicating with effectiveness and authority, we think it makes an apt acronym. It spells out six important tests to ensure that communicators do not fall into some of the most common mistakes we encounter:

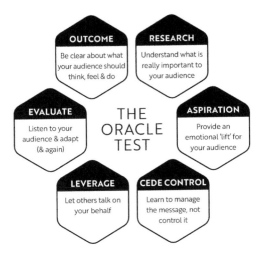

I. OUTCOME – Be clear about want what you your audience to think, feel and do

While it might offer a shot of dopamine, measuring the number of clicks, or 'likes', or the number of followers that you have on Twitter doesn't engage your audience. Thus, it isn't likely to influence how they think. So the first question we ask is, 'What is the outcome you seek from this communication?'

Elections aren't ultimately won on what people remember. They are won on the basis of a compelling story that encapsulates voters' interests and values… and ultimately captures their votes.

In the business world, marketing and advertising professionals have known for years that what you want to say is irrelevant; it is people's behaviour after they've heard you that is important. For example, how many cars have been sold as a result of communicating what the vehicle in question actually does? Not many. Selling cars is built on engaging people with the experience, lifestyle and sense of status that the car brings. These are all emotional attributes. The communications objective is simple: get people to choose their car, not a competitor's.

Logically, when it comes to communicating, it is vital that the planning starts with where you want to end up, and that should be about answering the question: 'what do I want people to think, feel and do as a result of my message?'

II. RESEARCH – Understand what is really important to your audience

Many leaders have slipped up by hearing and reciting pieces of research that reinforce their pre-existing point of view. The feeling predates the thought. It is uncomfortable to hear people say something different to what we think and feel. This explains people's well-worn aversion to discussions of politics, religion or money. With this in mind, we encourage leaders to really understand what matters most to their audience, how they see you and how they really feel.

In the world of 'big data', it's easy to get drawn into looking at the numbers – trying to extrapolate what they mean (or worse, using them to extrapolate a picture you want to see). Employee opinion surveys and elections polls are the very worst examples of this. They can use a thousand data points to tell you nothing at all. They are snapshots, not the full story. Understanding what is really important to your audience requires asking the right, provoking questions and listening to the replies – as well as the shifting sentiments underlying them. Not either or.

III. ASPIRATION - Provide an emotional 'lift' for your audience

As we have emphasised, we remain primarily emotionally-driven primates. As behavioural psychologists over recent decades have demonstrated, we are not merely 'rational calculating machines' but more so social, emotional, feeling beings. Innumerable studies have shown we are actually more active – and we accomplish more – when we are hopeful and optimistic. We are actually physically stronger through positive emotions compared to their negative counterparts. Thus, any truly compelling message needs to lift its audience. Smart communicators neglect this reality at their peril.

IV. CEDE CONTROL – Learn to manage the message, not control it

People in authority have always known the maxim that 'knowledge and information is power'. One of the biggest changes brought by the social media revolution has been the inexorable spread of knowledge and, in turn, the diffusion of power. While many of the old 'gatekeepers' remain, new sources of influence have sprung up all over the terrain. Communities are flexing their activist muscles in ways we haven't seen before. Do you know which ones you need to involve?

Not only does this have implications for your communication strategy, but also the precise lexicon you must use. Words and language have always mattered – they are becoming more precise and powerful than ever before. Without control and use of clear language, one risks misinterpretation and rumours running rife. It is those who have learned how to balance ceding control with managing the message who have been the most successful in the new age of campaigns and communications we now inhabit.

V. LEVERAGE – Let others talk on your behalf

We are surrounded by a plethora of accessible channels and potential audiences (or followers). One could quite literally spend all their time communicating online these days. In fact, some 200 million people do just that every day on Twitter, and if you are a teenager, then you're probably glued to your device for several hours every day. But success is not measured by 'likes'. Success is what happens as a result of your communication.

We trust people like ourselves more than we do remote leaders. As an example, Sophie Hinchliffe is an ex-hairdresser who began cheeringly filming herself while cleaning and showing off her new home. In two years, this unassuming 30-something from England has now transformed into 'Mrs Hinch', a 'super-influencer' with over four million followers on Instagram. Her so-called #hincharmy are so loyal that they mimic everything she does with an attitude of 'if it's good enough for Mrs Hinch, then it's good for me'. And that translates into real dollars.

In fact, 60% of people who have heard of her said that they would buy something that she recommends. Manufacturers cottoned on quick. Simply by having Mrs Hinch say a good word about a product, associated brands have seen their demand grow by over 300% in some cases.

What does this tell us? It is critical that you engage with the people who – to paraphrase from Heineken – will 'reach the parts of your audience landscape that others cannot'. New models of power mean that this is far less to do with coercion and capital than previously. Communicators with Nimblicity know how to use others' agendas without them necessarily being aware that they are helping you at all.

VI. EVALUATE – Listen to your audience and adapt (and again)

More than ever, you must listen, learn and 'sense check' against what you thought you had communicated. As our friend, the famous US pollster Frank Luntz put it memorably, "It's not what you say that matters… it's what they hear."

We've all been in the situation where the intended message sent is not the message that has been received. Before you have even taken your first sip of coffee, there is every chance that what you said will be traduced, (mis)translated and turned against you. Having an inbuilt mechanism of dispassionate evaluation (i.e. not simply checking Twitter) is critical if you are not to be obsolete by brunch time. Evaluation and re-evaluation are the best and only disciplines for retaining your vital agility and adaptability.

Conventional wisdom is to turn to the data to see if the message reached its intended audience and then listen to the assessment of those closest to us. Unless you have the equivalent of a Mafia *consigliere* at your side, be wary that most people will say what you want to hear and not what you need to hear. We'll talk more about this in Chapter 8, but real insight and evaluation require listening at a different level, a level where you are genuinely open to changing your mind and not simply thinking about the response you want to give.

New Zealand – 'End of Life Choice'

Politics truly is personal, and in 2019 one of the author's lost his father to an aggressive and incurable cancer. In the latter stages of the disease, while weak and ravaged but perfectly lucid about what the future held, he asked whether it would be possible 'to bring about terminus'. This is a situation and a question none of us wants to face. And yet, many of us will. So, it didn't feel such a coincidence when we were approached to manage a nascent 'Yes to Euthanasia' campaign in New Zealand the following year.

The issue would be put to a referendum, thanks largely to the efforts of two people: Matt Vickers, a Kiwi who campaigned movingly about his late wife Lecretia's battle with a terminal illness (and her right to die as she wished). Vickers was supported by

David Seymour, leader of a New Zealand party of one MP, who nonetheless managed to steer the necessary legislation through. Both worked tirelessly to push what at times seemed like a lost cause. They demonstrated just what one or two committed people can achieve with the right tenacity and drive.

The campaign would be a *much* harder slog than it first appeared. Although the 'Yes' vote started with a narrow polling advantage, the 'No' campaign remained the favourite. Almost everywhere euthanasia has been put to the public, it has been voted down. It is easy to scare people about the risks of 'killing off granny'. As an illustration, when the issue was put to public consultation, 90% of the submissions were opposed. Death is not a topic that average people enjoy discussing and debating at all, as research demonstrated from the off.

Meanwhile, the 'antis' would have a clear, ready-made base: the conservative/church-driven 'values voters' would form a solid and well-funded core upon which a broader public campaign could be built. We also had to manage the cross-currents of the recreational marijuana referendum that was (unhelpfully) being held on the same day. We would have to work hard *not* to be labelled thoughtless libertarians with no idea of the 'slippery slope' we were creating.

Using the ORACLE tests, the desired *outcome* would be for New Zealand to embrace euthanasia, and that required a clear campaign *objective* to score a simple '50% + 1' of the vote. We began intensive, deep research to understand *how* Kiwis thought about the issue with the help of an insightful behavioural psychologist, Briar Harland. We established that this wasn't a story about 'death' or terminal illness at all. It was about *choice*, *dignity* and *control*, more than anything else. This was how we could turn a subject so bleak into something positive and even *aspirational*. The vote would thus be framed not as 'euthanasia' at all… but End of Life Choice.

The focus groups and depth interviews we held were perhaps the most moving we had experienced. While we found that initially, people did *not* want to discuss the topic, when they did it brought out their most deeply held thoughts and beliefs on themselves and the people they loved… on *both* sides of the debate. Normally gruff men found themselves breaking down as they related their own personal stories. But what emerged was a strong sense of the *pride* and *dignity* people wanted to retain in their most vulnerable times; *compassion* for others who are suffering unnecessarily; and the *personal autonomy* that independent-minded New Zealanders felt was so important at the end of their lives.

The campaign itself followed a pattern we had predicted. The 'No' movement was better funded and used those resources to drive up the 'risks' of End of Life Choice: how could you be sure that this law wouldn't be used by unscrupulous relatives to drive vulnerable pensioners to their demise? Isn't *all* life sacred? Won't the law simply begin a 'slippery slope' to anyone wanting to top themselves, having just had a bad day? We might be outspent but would not be out-thought. We needed to have answers (or at least, responses) to each of these attacks and more. *Tone* would be important too – calming the more outlandish fears the other side was stoking while being clear that we respected the other point of view.

On the 17th of October 2020 in a vote delayed by the COVID-19 epidemic, New Zealand voted by a massive margin – 65% to 34% – for the legalisation of euthanasia. On the same day, marijuana legalisation was voted *down* by 51% to 49%.

Paying attention to the surrounding *context*, the campaign had successfully distanced itself from an issue – recreational marijuana – that Kiwis found *less* attractive the more they studied it. It had overcome a rich, ruthless, and disciplined opponent. Most importantly, the country had chosen to *empower* its citizens when they would need it the most. Rather than suffering the twin anguish of incurable disease and the denial of personal agency, Kiwis will now have the right to go at the moment of *their* choosing. With appropriate safeguards in place (the law only applies to the most severely ill and those who can demonstrate their independence of mind), potentially hundreds of thousands could now see their pain and discomfort eased in their moment of need. A fitting tribute to Lecretia Seales and to Dad.

BrewDog and the disgruntled employees

When friends James Watt and Martin Dickie started bottling beer and selling it from the back of a van in 2007, they would never imagine that their company would hit the headlines for all the wrong reasons 14 years later. With its 'anti-business' business model, BrewDog grew rapidly by doing things differently. From raising finance through their 'Equity for Punks' crowdfunding to their irreverent marketing approach, their intent has been to grow their business by putting BrewDog at the heart of a *community* that shares their passion for beer and doing things differently. And with this approach, they have built a £250 million global business that is now one of the top 20 most valuable beer brands in the world.

What could possibly go wrong?

From workplace bullying, harassment, and lack of diversity to gender equality, the discussion about issues in the workplace has been around for many years and taken even more prominence as a result of social campaigns such as #MeToo. On the 9th of June 2021, an open letter from around 250 former and current employees was published on Twitter that didn't pull its punches and described the alleged 'toxic culture' at the company and singling out James Watt personally. The media firestorm that emerged certainly tarnished the reputation of both the co-founders and the brand itself.

Only time will tell if the damage is lasting.

Initially, Watt said that the company categorically refuted everything suggested in the employee letter. However, within a week, he had changed his tune and accepted that the buck stopped with him and that "in the hard and fast environment of high growth, I have all too often neglected many important people elements of our business."

James Watt isn't the first, nor will he be the last leader who, by being so focused on the business objectives, simply stopped paying attention to what was happening around him. The result being that his initial communication was ill-judged, and his *mea culpa* was probably too little too late to save his own skin. In the # era, it isn't just old ways of doing things that are undone by 'moving fast and breaking things'. Reputations decades in the making can be undone with a few clicks in a matter of seconds.

Which way next? The age of millennials and molecules

In so much of the opinion research that we do, we detect a yearning for a deeper nourishment from respondents. Concepts that may have sounded like buzzwords or anachronisms in the 1980s and 90s – community, character, connection – have achieved new *salience*, precisely as they have been redefined by social media.

While we remain divided along lines – both real and imagined – of race, region or religion, none is quite so stark (nor politically predictive) as that of *age*. Brexit, Trump and the populist insurgents of recent years depended on the votes of the baby boomers. Millennials (and their even younger cohorts) tend to be outward-looking, optimistic and open-minded. Newspapers spill over with 'lifestyle' opinion polls that show that the under-35s actually have *less* sex and *more* expectations. They struggle with higher debt and lower wages than the generation before. They will, most likely, be the first generation to earn less than their predecessors.

Today in focus groups and workshops, it is still quite common to hear those same predecessors bemoan the 'poor work ethic' and Instagram superficiality of their younger comrades. There is, as we shall see, a *bit* of truth in these claims – but not a lot. The 'inter-generational warfare' idea is better for clickbait than credible opinion analysis. The rate of demographic change and education explain attitudes to party and race as much as age. But there are vital, qualitative differences with this demographic.

So, what are some of the differences that hit you when interviewing a group of millennials? Perhaps most striking are the similarities in attitudes, whether in Alabama or Australia. They will get many of the same videos and cultural references in a way that just wasn't possible before the internet. They are more individual and non-ideological than other, similar-sized groups. They are flexible and fluid in their approach. They prioritise the personal over the political and economic; emphasising environmental, economic and social justice over the more traditional staples of 'growth and jobs'. A direct legacy of their 'coming of age' in the aftershocks of the 2008/09 worldwide economic earthquake is that they are more cheerfully open about their economic insecurity. They prioritise the experiential (world travel, say) over the economic (such as home ownership).

Are the under-35s the most narcissistic generation yet? Some 60% of millennials agree with the statement, 'I will be famous someday', and the number rises with the next generation ('Generation I', or the under-25s). Two thirds of college students expect, somewhat optimistically, to become millionaires someday while freely admitting that they have cheated in exams. At the same time, depression and anxiety have *sky rocketed* among the same generation, in spite of other risk factors – such as alcohol and drugs – *falling* during the same period. So, they may well be the most aspirational cohort we have yet researched and studied… but they are also the most anxious.

The economic aspect of this unease may have something to do with the highly visible inequality they have faced in the past decade. COVID-19 has only increased the gap between the well-off and the 'essential' workers they publicly applaud. Calls for 'fairness' and 'a levelling of the playing field' have replaced the priorities of 'prudence', 'pocketbooks' and 'personal responsibility'.

Well over half of US millennials now say they would prefer a 'socialist' economic system to that of a capitalist one, rising to fully two thirds of Democrats. By contrast, only one in three endorse the free-market basis of a Western economic model. Some armchair political pundits would argue that this is simply a political truism – 'Younger people always tilt left'. Only it isn't. Both Margaret Thatcher and Ronald Reagan won healthy majorities among 20- and 30-somethings. Later, Joe Biden very nearly matched the GOP's advantage among older voters. Beware parroting the conventional wisdom – pay attention to what is *really* going on.

An audience grown distrusting and disdainful...

While our day-to-day 'wants' and 'issues' resemble the weather of passing showers, the underlying public *mood* is more like the long-term climate that underpins it. According to Harris' annual 'Happiness Study', *two thirds* of Americans report that they are, broadly speaking, unhappy. Think about that for a second. Sixty-seven per cent of people living in the world's most 'advanced' economy are flat-out miserable. Consider that the most fundamental question that pollsters ask – "Are we heading in the right direction, or pretty seriously off on the wrong track?" for instance – underpins *everything* about how we think, talk and make decisions. This perceived need to 'change course' was brought to the fore visibly and viscerally by the victories of Trump and Brexit, the sheer sentiment overpowering the strong arguments against both.

It is impossible to point directly at a single root cause of this malaise. But some of the research work we do helps to illuminate the terrain. Firstly, trust is dying at the 'macro' level of big organisations and institutions: big businesses, big government, big NGOs, big politicians… 'big' anything, in fact, is routinely greeted by a mixture of distrust and disdain. Edelman's 'Trust Barometer' shows how far trust has plunged since the Global Financial Crisis, with a brief recovery in a few countries adjudged to have handled COVID-19 'well'. In the words of Edelman themselves;

> *"The [2019] Barometer reveals that trust has changed profoundly in the past year – people have shifted their trust to the relationships within their control, most notably their employers."*

At the same time, what you cannot help but notice – if you are interviewing and interrogating the voters and employees of the world every night – is that people are *struggling*. This is not simply 'inequality' (that too is a rising concern). After two global crises in a decade, the level of world debt is at the highest it has ever been and it is still rising. For instance, the average Briton spends £105 for every £100 that they earn. European economies have seen youth unemployment stuck at double-digit levels for a dozen years. In human terms, the struggles people endure to simply feed and clothe their families is heart-rending. Chinese debt levels are at unsustainably high levels too, at *hundreds* of trillions of dollars with an increasingly bellicose leadership. People sense that the West is woefully unprepared for the next crisis – financial or military. Is it any wonder that we're anxious?

... Not to mention *disengaged*

Much of our British research demonstrates huge disengagement at work, and there is strong suspicion that this has much to do with our country's lamentable productivity numbers. Undoubtedly, poor communication contributes to this. In our experience, bigger companies tend to fall back on age-old practices because it is simply too difficult for them to change a lifetime of bad habits. We live in a 'post-talking points' world, and yet many communicators still insist on talking to their colleagues as if they were taking a school assembly.

Addressing this begins with Emotional Intelligence, one of the recurrent themes of Nimblicity.

Employees have become smarter and more sceptical about internal communications. Whereas once, perhaps, they would've engaged with a discussion about 'brand values', internal audiences are much quicker to ask, 'what's in it for me?' The transactional and *tangible*. As one gruff retail employee put it recently, "I don't want to hear about your grand strategy. Tell me how I can make more money – or one day, have my boss' job…" This deeper need for purpose, for principle, is something that has risen in lock step with the primacy of the *individual*. Today, we feel more at ease discussing our most profound needs. Thus, Nimblicity is also about the communication of the intensely *personal*.

A company as the backbone of their community

As well as incubating and inculcating a sense of community, politicians could learn a thing or two from some companies in acting as the fulcrum of communities.

Smith's Food & Drug is the kind of place that 'the other America' shops. Middle-class Americans living in the so-called 'Flyover States', between the self-regarding centres of East and West Coasts. They aren't flashy. The little things count; they will wait for tomatoes to go 'on special' or will stock up on salsa when the stock gets reduced by 10%. 'Friendly Freebie Fridays' are more than a cute bit of alliterative advertising; they're the essential difference between a weekly shop that stays a few bucks within your weekly budget – and one that exceeds it.

A British person visiting a Smith's Food & Drug in the American Midwest would be struck by a sense of the familiar. The family-owned store chain has much in common with an average Tesco, ASDA or Sainsbury's. We had the privilege of working for Smith's through their smart and savvy Communications chief, Keith Daley. The company decided to take a courageous stand on customers' behalf against credit card giant Visa's unilateral hiking of their fees. Although Visa assumed the increase would be passed on wordlessly, Smith's knew that even a 2–3% hit could make all the difference to those who shop there. They decided to make a noise about it.

What struck so forcefully during our research was not so much that shoppers depend on their supermarkets for so much more than low prices – that, perhaps, isn't news. It was also the sense of shared struggle. While the American ideal of 'community' with its Parent–Teacher Associations (PTAs), bowling leagues and Ned Flanders 'good neighbourliness' has been eroded... so have the margins that the middle-class lives its life by. One friendly, rotund mom-of-four elicited quiet murmurs of approval when she said, "Shopping smart... coupons, specials and one-off deals, over time these little things really make a big difference. They put a bit of control in OUR hands again." While people feel ever-decreasing autonomy over the forces controlling their lives, this is a big deal.

Customers' scepticism and suspicion towards big businesses doesn't stop with grocery chains. Local bricks 'n mortar stores have important, positive points of difference with their 'click-to-order' rivals, which they have barely begun to explore. The faceless, offshore-headquartered world of 'Big Tech' and 'Big Finance' embodies everything about 'old power' (which we shall explore in more detail in Chapter 9). They model command-and-control power with a noticeably narrow (and usually opaque) governance structure. Often, the very top is concealed in some distant, highly tax-efficient offshore location.

At the same time, there is something oddly 'New Power' about companies like Smith's. They are firmly embedded in the *communities* they serve. They value transparency. They actively treat customers as real people and partners, not profit-maximising automatons who may as well be an algorithm for all the shared intimacy and warmth in relations. We are coming full circle.

Businesses like Smith's – and their parent company Kroger – actually have a considerable amount of political capital, which they often don't maximise. This may be a legacy of being seen for years by some as 'the bad guys' of capitalism – a thriving business. But the world is evolving fast. Consumers, politicians, shareholders, suppliers and employees are as interested in *how* you do business now. It is interesting to speculate what businesses like Smith's could accomplish if they positioned themselves more as stakeholders in their communities, rather than simply 'customer servers'. This could be far more potent than many brands' paltry and outdated 'Corporate Social Responsibility' efforts.

What are 'community values' in practice?

One sunny afternoon, moderating a focus group, deep in country New South Wales, Australia, a working-class dad happened to mention that he had not worked for a few months. Upon asking him why that was, we were told that he'd been in rehab. After a nasty injury on a building site, one of two jobs he needed to keep up his mortgage and all the outgoings you'd associate with three children, he'd become addicted to painkillers, which then gradually descended into a flown-blown opioid addiction. He had ended up a petty thief, selling his kids' toys to feed his habit. This very nearly cost him his family in the process. But he'd been lucky. His wife had supported him through the addiction ordeal, and his children had stuck by him. He'd recently celebrated two months clean. As he finished telling his story, the group broke into spontaneous applause. This is assuredly *not* a common occurrence in a political focus group...

This story – and that reaction – could have been the same in Britain, or almost anywhere in the United States, Canada or *dozens* of other countries in 2021/22. As we become increasingly individualised in the way we live our lives, the struggles we face are *remarkably* similar. And so are our responses. Accepting that there are pockets of intolerance everywhere – and always will be – our societies show remarkably more empathy and sympathy. Notably, more so than was the case even a couple of decades ago. We *overwhelmingly* accept the right of people to live and love how they wish. That 'families' can come in myriad forms – and should be celebrated as such... and that the 'War on Drugs' has been an overwhelming failure, in drastic need of a policy overhaul and a fresh, compassionate approach (which is what underpinned that Australian applause). The point here is not to list *every* convergence in our values, but just to note they are occurring.

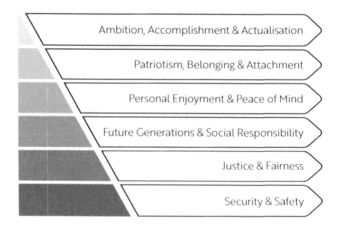

Ambition, Accomplishment & Actualisation

Patriotism, Belonging & Attachment

Personal Enjoyment & Peace of Mind

Future Generations & Social Responsibility

Justice & Fairness

Security & Safety

Whether the 'community' in question is a business, charity, parish council or country, *community value systems* are remarkably similar. Whether you are addressing a global business, an electorate or nation, a community will, logically, prioritise its values. A simple overview might look something like this:

I. Security & safety

My – and my family's – security and well being. Both in a financial sense, as well as our physical security. This is what 'the economy' means in relevant terms: will you keep my job? Will my kids be safe on the street? Are we going to be able to put food on the table and fuel in the car?

II. Justice & fairness

Our sense that the rules are right and fair – and being properly enforced to the benefit of all. The sense that 'the system is rigged against our people... the powerful will beat up those who can't defend themselves... and the elites of media and politics look down on you' is indeed corrosive. If you allow it to take hold, nothing much else you say will matter.

III. Future generations & social responsibility

We change when we have children. The world we are leaving behind for our kids' rockets up our values system. And this can equate to anything from the environment to the employment market we are leaving behind us. Lazy thinking tends to label 'social justice warriors' as only the tattooed 20-somethings glueing themselves to tube trains. In fact, new parents often share their concerns... if not their methods.

IV. Personal enjoyment & peace of mind

Our personal experience matters more than at any time in history. From the Pyramids to Pearl Harbour, human history has been defined by collective endeavour. And while this still cuts through – we could hardly be more aware of the world we live in. We see it through the lens of the personal. We need our part to be recorded. We need to find happiness; personal meaning in the mundane and day-to-day. In short, we need to *matter*.

V. Patriotism, belonging & attachment

Group attachment still resonates as much, if not more than, personal self-interest. What sets us apart? What positively differentiates us from 'the rest'? This could be American military types distancing themselves from the war hero-bashing Trump. A team or unit within a big business conglomerate. Or 'mums' banding together to form a lobby group. Our attachment (and need for it) to tribe is as strong as when our ancestors emerged from the African savannah.

VI. Ambition, accomplishment & actualisation

Although much has been misunderstood since Maslow published his famous 'hierarchy of needs', self-actualisation is really about *integration*. As humans, we all have egos and ambitions which need to be met. At the same time, deeply buried spiritual and emotional drivers will emerge as we mature and – if we don't face them – become the most effective instruments of our own self-sabotage. In the end, figuring all this out and learning to live with life's paradoxes becomes the whole point.

Taking politics as an example, this order follows a remorseless logic. If you have won the argument on security ('growth and jobs', say, in terms of national politics), then you can progress to an argument over 'fairness' and social justice. If not – as the 2019

British general election illustrated – you are *highly* unlikely to be trusted by your audience, no matter how incompetent those in power may prove to be.

This proves to be just as true within companies and other large organisations. As we have seen, employees can be willing to accept even quite draconian cuts to jobs and conditions *if* you can clearly demonstrate that it's in the longer-term interests of everybody's financial well being. When you 'own' security, you have permission to be believed on fairness and future generations.

Similarly, if you are attempting to sell a story of 'tomorrow's impossibly exciting new future' and 'the sky's the limit' in the next century… do not be surprised if you are met by incredulous scepticism from an audience that perceives that you're not able to maintain basic 'health & safety' procedures. When you communicate through *the lens of your values* – explaining *why* you are doing, ahead of *what* you are doing – you become *immeasurably* more credible with your audience. So, understanding your community's hierarchy of values is vital if you are to communicate with them effectively – and take them with you on your journey.

If we are living in an age of more conscious, communal attachment, we would argue that that is a very good thing in its own right. But the opposing view is predictable and still prevalent: there is no such thing as community or society. Businesses are profit-maximising machines, and so long as they stay within the law, they are best when they stick to just that. So-called 'Corporate Social Responsibility' (CSR) programmes are, at best, a misguided use of shareholders' money. At worst, they are dangerous and driven by vanity. We don't disagree. But we are talking about something deeper than 'CSR'.

The rebirth of the concept of *community* is as much a part of our shifting context today as the ideas of privatisation and innovation were of Reagan and Thatcher 40 years ago. Or workers' rights, welfare provision and pensions were in the Progressive Era a century ago. Back then, well-funded opposition to progressive legislation was mounted by vast, private oligopolies in oil, the railroads, banks and many other industries deemed 'too big to fail'. They attempted to ignore the tide of history and saw themselves broken up by a newly assertive citizenry. The 'Big Tech' ad giants of today should feel that they are on notice.

'Paying attention' means sticking close

Successful companies and political parties in the age of Nimblicity will be those who have an *acute* understanding of the communities they serve. Successful leaders will be those who build and depend upon mechanisms of engagement with the communities they serve.

Yes, they will be listening intently, but also focused on enabling people to take responsibility – in service of a cause greater than themselves. Without naivety, they will not rely on the power structures of old and instead will seek to build new, creative coalitions of communities. And they will see such a broader, peer-driven approach not as a threat but as a huge opportunity to drive lasting, credible and people-powered change.

Of the Fortune 500 companies 50 years ago, *only around one in ten survives* on that list today. Whether a corporation or sports coach, yesterday's innovator or 'Special One' is tomorrow's obsolete dinosaur. And like our primordial ancestors, those who survive and succeed into the next generation – that diminishing minority – are those with the keenest ears to the ground. Pay attention to what is happening around you.

LAW OF NIMBLICITY #2:

DARE TO BE DIFFERENT, AND AVOID FAILING CONVENTIONALLY

"We judge more by the eye than by the hand, for everyone can see and few can feel. Everyone sees what you appear to be, few really know what you are."

Niccolò Machiavelli, political consultant

We are all becoming leaders now. As you ascend through the ranks of an organisation — be it a community group, NGO, company or local sports team — problems of increasing complexity become your responsibility. In so doing, it can be tempting to fall back on certain, trusty 'truisms'… when in reality, there are few such things. As Oracle co-founder Larry Ellison put it pithily, "the only way to get ahead is to find errors in conventional wisdom." Don't be one of the majority who are more comfortable with 'failing conventionally' than the stigma of standing out from the crowd, even if that means succeeding.

(The) Queen's greatest hits

In our experience – whether working for some of the world's biggest multilateral organisations or managing electoral campaigns – it is the *technical* problems that are often the most straightforward to solve. Once a process is fixed, it should stay fixed. People are different. And the way we communicate – exchange information, thoughts and feelings – is undergoing a revolution. This change is placing a whole new set of demands on communicators, for which the old games of 'Command and Control', 'Hitting Your Key Messages' and 'Spin Control' are growing obsolete.

For instance, how often have you seen in public life or encountered in your day-to-day working life one of the following scenarios?

- The person at the top of the team or organisation doesn't appear to know *what they actually want to do*. Uncertain of their own ultimate purpose. The legacy they want to be known for when they move on. Their words are fine-sounding and fresh, but there is no clear direction, no palpable change in view from their predecessors, and no vision that their employees would 'die in a ditch' for?

- An experienced politician running for office, with seemingly abundant qualifications and qualities, loses out to a comparative greenhorn. The commentators and critics exclaim their disbelief whilst telling us these inexplicable happenings are 'black swan' events – one-offs – and yet… they just keep happening.

- A great initiative begins with a great message, well-communicated, and then… nothing happens. It can seem as though only the small, originating team of three or four can even remember what the point was. And they are just left 'spinning their wheels'.

- A new employee joins your team excited, motivated, and full of new ideas. Then as the days turn into months, the energy and enthusiasm they walked through the door with plateaus and then plummets. Before too long, they are, but another demotivated drone, checking their social media feeds (and jobs searches) all the while being increasingly – and maddeningly – difficult to get rid of.

Just spend a few hours reading the numerous posts on LinkedIn, and you'll soon see that many are obsessed with using technology to connect better with their audiences. Technology is changing the way we communicate – and we will look at the consequences of this in more detail in Chapter 4. But it's important to remember that this is not a new phenomenon. Just look at what television did in the 1950s and, in particular, the British Royal family.

After Queen Elizabeth II gave a speech to workers at the Jaguar car factory in 1956, she was publicly criticised by the Tory peer Lord Altrincham for being out of touch with the public. He suggested the monarchy must adapt to the more liberal post-war society. After Prime Minister Harold Macmillan warned her of the trend for nations to abolish their monarchies, the Queen agreed to televise her royal Christmas message for the first time in 1957. In her broadcast, she said, "it's inevitable that I should seem a rather remote figure to many of you… who never really touches your personal lives. But now, at least for a few minutes, I welcome you to the peace of my own home."

Fast-forward to her 2017 Christmas message, and the Queen said:

"Sixty years ago today, a young woman spoke about the speed of technological change as she presented the first television broadcast of its kind. She described the moment as a landmark. Six decades on, the presenter has 'evolved' somewhat, as has the technology she described. Back then, who could have imagined that people would one day be watching this on laptops and mobile phones – as some of you are today."

What Queen Elizabeth II quickly learnt in 1956 is that when it came to connecting with her audience, she could not continue to apply the conventional wisdom of the time. Namely, leaders and the 'elites' of society had communicated purely on a need-to-know basis.

And while a novel technology then gave the Queen the means to reach millions – now *billions* of people worldwide – her real breakthrough in the 1950s was adapting with Nimblicity to the mood of her audience. They didn't want to be communicated to on a 'need-to-know' basis… they wanted to *know*.

Despite being a good role model for Nimblicity and putting aside conventional communications wisdom, it would be putting it mildly to say that the Palace hasn't always got things right. The days after the death of Diana, Princess of Wales, are an example of the royal family failing to demonstrate Nimblicity. Newspaper headlines at the time confirmed that they badly misjudged public opinion; they were slow off the mark connecting at an *emotional* level with the British people.

Start with the heart

Leadership means more than protecting or directing people. It depends on the ability to inspire and engage, especially – and this is the important part – *those who might not ordinarily agree with you.* This element of leadership demands an extraordinary level of emotional intelligence. This is why it is so much easier to conjure eye-rolling examples of people who are bad at it than those rare beasts who can 'sway' a room. As the poet and US civil rights activist Maya Angelou put it, "They will forget what you say, but they will never forget how you made them feel."

How many times have you been to a PowerPoint presentation, bombarded with facts, figures and data… and left feeling somehow as though you know less than when it began? We have been conditioned in our working lives to 'make the case' for what we want others to do. Sure, you have to have a case for spending money or making an investment… but an over-reliance on this tried-and-tested approach simply doesn't cut through today. Instagram's Mrs Hinch doesn't make a rational argument through a business case for her Hinch Army to buy a new cleaning product. Instead, she touches their aspirational (and therefore emotional) needs by showing them what it can do for them.

There are no more decisive, important emotions than those of hope for change and fear of loss. And from *Star Wars* to *Saving Private Ryan*, the filmmaking industry knows that when we engage with a story of hope, we're hooked – and they'll have a blockbuster on their hands. In the end, we are storytelling creatures. *People don't buy 'key messages'; they buy stories.* And storytelling isn't some new buzzword or technique; it's hard-wired into our brains. Compared to other primates, our hippocampus (learning and memory) facility is rather small, while our (stress-producing) adrenal gland is too large. Stories — narratives that mirror the neural networks in our heads — are our first line of defence against a hostile world.

A good strategy is a good story

Stories continue to fulfil their ancient function of binding society by reinforcing a set of common values and strengthening the ties of *authentic* connection. But stories also have another benefit in the modern world. They allow us to make sense of otherwise unfathomable amounts of data. We absorb far more than our rational mind can possibly keep up with, so stories provide us with 'short-cuts' in order to cope.

Of course, this rapid simplification can cause problems with complicated issues such as the debate about whether to leave the European Union or a business communicating 'transformational change'. The risk is that the arguments get diluted down to the point that they are meaningless. But turn your message into a credible and compelling *story*, and this will give you a priceless advantage in campaigns and communications. Because of our genetics, your audience becomes engaged because their emotional networks are aroused – namely their hopes, hatred, anxieties, anger, enthusiasm or enjoyment. People rarely act based upon lists of information, facts or 'key messages'. It is the *emotions* these things provoke that count. We behave based upon the stories we hear – even, or especially, subconsciously. This is a fundamental cornerstone of Nimblicity explored in depth in Chapter 6. But first, let's look at a real-life case study.

Nike and storytelling

Nelson Farris stands about six feet tall, with a Tom Selleck moustache and the trim build of someone who ran track in college. Nelson happened to be one of the very first people to be hired by Nike's founder Phil Knight in the early seventies, promoting and selling Nike shoes out of his car. Nike's name is 'borrowed' from the Greek goddess of victory, and over five decades, Farris estimates he has held 20 different jobs during his Nike career, travelling well over a million miles while visiting more than 50 countries on six continents. With no intention of slowing down, he is currently Director of Corporate Education or more informally known as Nike's Chief Storyteller.

It may surprise many that such a well-known brand would employ someone with such an 'off-the-wall' role, but it's more common than many people realise. General Electric deployed Ronald Reagan in a very similar job (from 1954–62), touring the company's factories and plants, all the while meticulously developing one of the most influential speeches of the 20th century. Nelson Farris' job isn't so political, but it's every bit as inspirational as 'the great communicator's'. And it's critical to a brand like Nike that lives its brand promise 'inside out'.

If employee engagement numbers started to drop or sales were sagging, in would fly Nelson to remind them why they were there and how it all started by sharing his personal stories of working with Phil Knight and selling the sneakers out of the trunk of his car at track and field events.

Nike noticed that the immensely likeable Farris' visits had a significant effect on the company wherever he went. Employee engagement, productivity and sales all went up. By being a living embodiment of Nike's unique corporate culture, employees loved it. They were inspired by listening to him in a way they never would be to some corporate, Mitt Romney type (sorry, Mitt).

The reason? Because Nelson had the credibility of being there from the beginning and experiencing the ups and downs like them. He had been there, done that and got the T-shirt for almost every challenge or opportunity people were facing. Not many people could say they'd been in the room when Weiden and Kennedy turned 'Just Do It' into a living, breathing reality.

Only Nelson could be honest – sometimes brutally so – about the company's failures, such as the ill-fated attempt to become a fashion and not sports brand in the 1970s. He wouldn't hold back and had the courage to call things out. Like Reagan, his secret was almost that there was no secret. He was one of them, and he would've had no quarrels with Reagan's notion that, "I'd never talk 'down' to them… or 'up' to them, in fact. I'd never want to separate myself from ordinary Americans in that way."

So, whether you are telling a fairy story to a five-year-old or pitching to be president, any good storyteller knows that the first ingredient is credibility, and the second ingredient is empathising with your audience. And it really helps if you like the person spinning the yarn, too.

But Nelson isn't the only storyteller at Nike. The company is blessed with other great storytellers and frequently uses the sporting legends who endorse its products to share their own personal stories of achievement to inspire both customers and employees.

If Phil Knight was the first person to know everything about Nike's products inside out, then it wouldn't be long before it would need others to have the same zealous passion and knowledge for the products. In 1981, the EKIN Program was established to ensure that the passion for the product held by the likes of Phil Knight and Nelson Farris would pass on to a new generation of disciples. People who had such detailed knowledge of the latest Nike products that they could talk about them inside out and back to front – hence EKIN being NIKE spelt backwards.

But not anyone can be an EKIN at Nike. There is a tough selection process that requires candidates to present something that demonstrates their passion. They're not 'Internal Communications' people; they weren't corporate ambassadors or trained PR types, with a pre-written script. They were not necessarily especially senior in the business.

Those looking for the next EKINS are looking for people who are brilliant at telling stories and capable of going into a Nike store, factory or office and talking with authority and passion about the materials and stories behind the latest products for an upcoming season. It is the EKIN's job to go out into the world and tell the story of that product: how it came about, who dreamed up the critical new features that customers are raving about, the need that it serves.

And those that succeed become part of a unique club of storytellers at Nike, and that includes having the obligatory Nike 'swoosh' tattoo to prove it.

So, the EKINS are as much a part of the incredible brand definition and distinction that Nike has today as any marketing plan. Brands need heart and soul – they need a story – and those things are provided by people like Nelson Farris and the EKINS. One more thing. This approach to storytelling by Nike also proved to be highly significant in overcoming the risk of a complete breakdown of trust (such as with the South-East Asian workshop practices discussed elsewhere in this book). Brand narratives are meaningless unless they are backed up with accompanying *action*.

A business that practises good, transparent, authentic (and accountable) storytelling, is one that has purchased a valuable insurance policy for itself. Conventional wisdom is to *not* let go of the control of your message at any cost.

We'll talk more about the perils of doing this in Chapter 10. The experience at Nike has proved that by using stories and empowering others to share them, you are able to create even more power in your message and unleash an *emotional* connection with your audience that creates an unstoppable force. Nike took a real chance when they did this. It was 'off-script', unconventional and brave. And that's exactly why it worked.

If they can't feel it... don't use it

Elections, meanwhile, are about competing stories. Having managed election campaigns in dozens of countries, we are asked many times, 'How can you possibly understand the intricacies of this specific state… or that contentious national issue?' The answer is that the *emotional* narrative of any election is more important than any issue or policy. How we vote is driven by how we *feel* about the world, not facts and formulae or even policy and politics.

None of us likes to think of ourselves as predictable. And this is especially the case in the realm of politics. We much prefer to believe that we prioritise the intellectual over the instinctual, and yet, hardly any of our decision-making is rational at all. In fact, it is possible to predict our partisan choices 84% of the time, regardless of any 'factual' influence or information that we receive. This little-understood, neurological aspect of politics is fascinating, not least because it gives the lie to the idea that votes for Brexit or Trump were 'stolen' by Russian interference. What was really going on was a significant shift in the tides of public opinion. This trend is really far more interesting (if not to conspiracy theorists) to anyone who has a need to engage with people more deeply. But you have to be willing to think *differently.*

We are still really at the very beginning of our understanding of how we process emotional 'data': the impact of a candidate's (or indeed the CEO's) smile, image, body language and tone of voice, all of which we absorb and process *in a second* before they have even finished their first sentence. And yet, all the data suggests that these cues are every bit as influential on the vote as any policy gambit.

To us, this is why the low public esteem in which our politicians are held is grotesquely unfair. It is an immensely difficult task to run for and win office and requires enormous reserves of emotional (and intellectual) intelligence. After all, there is an infinite number of stories potential politicians could tell, but it is the speaker with the most *accurate-feeling* story who will be the one to win their audience. Conversely, the political spin doctor or strategist who says, 'we got 'em beat on the issues" tends to be the kind who becomes an expert in drafting concession speeches. Elections are – first and last – about voters' feelings.

The neuroscientist Drew Westen uses the example of America's contentious abortion debate to illustrate this further. In *The Political Brain,* he uses the language of the liberal left with that of the religious right to highlight the point about the importance of feelings. On the left, the argument of 'the right to choose' contrasts with that of the right, the messaging of 'partial birth abortions'. There is simply no contest as to which is more emotive and which, therefore, has struck more of a chord with the electorate. His central point was clear: politicians have it wrong when they see elections as contests of policy platforms alone; instead, look to the *emotive* resonance of your language.

Westen breaks down voters' thought process in an election into distinct, neurological stages, and they are worth remembering for our purposes. We have also found that the same thought processes can be applied outside of politics, with profit and non-profit organisations and their leaders:

1. How do I feel about a candidate and their principles?

2. How do they make me feel?

3. How do I feel about their personal characteristics... particularly their integrity, leadership and sense of justice?

4. How do I feel about their stance on issues that matter to me?

Based on our insights from dozens of election campaigns, these key questions have remained consistent and tellingly so. Recent years have seen a steady decline in the 'automatic' loyalty of people to a particular party. So, there are more prominent cleavages in politics today than 'left vs right'; for instance, age and levels of educational attainment were likely to be better predictors of support of Brexit, Trump and similar parties, such as the Swedish Democrats, or One Nation in Australia. What unites all of them is an appeal to voters' collective sense of tribe and community, a visual and linguistic approach that says s/he is 'one of us'.

When we feel part of a community, we feel safe.

When things get muddled...

It's fair to say that America's 3.5 million Muslims have had a torrid time since 9/11. A relatively tiny portion of the US population – at less than 1% of the total – nonetheless, since the time of Al Qaeda's grotesque attack, they have assumed an ever more perilous place in the American psyche. This has real, knock-on effects. Nearly 48% of American Muslims live at or below the poverty line. Rather than help, their neighbours tend to be suspicious, fed toxic scare stories by both the media and a president exploiting those fears by singling Muslims out for 'a complete and total shutdown' of migration to the US. Islamophobic attacks are up nationwide by 186% in 2019, and the depressing trend is to keep on spiralling upwards.

So, the 'American Muslims For Us All' (AM4USA) campaign was addressing a clear and present need. It was well-funded, too. One or two billionaires had given the campaign's founder, an ambitious political staffer called Samar Ali, enough hard cash to 'seed fund' the operation for a year or two at least, by which time a full-time fundraising operation could've been built. Volunteers were not hard to come by either, both from within the community itself and from student campuses buzzing with the energy and enthusiasm necessary for a really successful 'start up'. The campaign would be based out of Nashville, Tennessee, right in the middle of the Bible Belt – so pretty much the heart of the action as far as a religious dust-up was concerned.

The problems began at the very top. What were we trying to do? The businessmen who funded the initial outfit believed that the answer to Islamic poverty was to focus on business and commerce. Recent arrivals to a new country are not necessarily looking for a hand-out but – in the case of the entrepreneurial United States – a hand up. So, the objective would be primarily to facilitate introductions between local chambers of commerce and local Muslim-owned businesses or entrepreneurs looking to make a start.

So far, so good.

But a month or two down the road, conventional wisdom resulted in the campaign switching tack. Results were not as quick as AM4USA would have hoped, and so a decision was taken that nothing would change unless the media narrative around Muslims changed. So, media training sessions were scheduled for the campaign's ambassadors (leading Islamic lights in their local communities), who would be re-tasked, away from the commercial agenda and towards getting media to speak on behalf of the Muslim community in their area. On the plus side, a metric was easily available – the number of 'media hits' the campaign generated would be easily targeted and tracked.

Then it changed again. The campaign director decided that the Muslim community should model their approach on the way the Jewish community have built influence with a powerful presence in Washington, DC. Not unreasonably, she argued that the campaign should be the body to make that 'strategic shift' and that it would be like the Anti-Defamation League (set up to track down, and fight, cases of anti-semitism in America and all across the globe). While it wasn't overtly 'Jewish', it was established and controlled by Jews and hugely advantaged and protected the Jewish community. Why shouldn't the Muslim community enjoy a similar cheerleader?

And so, the objectives changed again, this time along with the name. 'American Muslims' was considered too divisive, and some focus groups had queried whether any non-Muslims could or would join a campaign with 'that word' in the title. So, 'American Muslims 4 Us All' turned into 'Millions of Conversations'. A third 'rebranding' in less than a year.

The point here is not to criticise what was a well-intentioned effort but to illustrate the harm that not answering the simplest of questions can bring. What do you exist for? What is your core purpose?

The lesson learned from AM4USA is that each and every objective change (and there were more) demanded a strategic shift – a new story and new skills. Significant chunks of money that had been spent on public opinion research were wasted. After all, what people expected and wanted from a business-focused campaign was considerably different to one dealing with the legal aspects of defamation and hate speech. Employee morale – that crucial intangible of every campaign, especially those that require a large number of volunteers – started to fade. And donors began moving away to other, more understandable causes.

AM4USA quite neatly encapsulates one of the biggest but least understood threats to a communications campaign, which is simply: all the things you could do. It takes real discipline to first take the strategic decisions on what your objectives are and where you will focus. But it takes even more grit to stick to them, especially when the going gets harder and people question your decisions to your face.

'Paralysis by analysis' or continually zig-zagging between one path and another has spelt doom for thousands of other well-funded, well-resourced campaigns.

Images Trump words

In the 1930s, the Nazi Party in Germany made spectacular use of the films of Leni Riefenstahl to make an unmatched emotional appeal to German voters exhausted by military defeat, humiliating reparations and weak leadership. Her stunning films, not only of political rallies but also the spectacle of Berlin's 1936 Olympic Games, spoke unmistakably to themes of pride, order, renaissance and – above all – national strength.

In a comparison from the modern era, President Ronald Reagan and Australian Prime Minister Paul Keating achieved a similar (albeit far more modest) effect by never appearing for set-piece, political events without their carefully chosen staging of a podium backed by a deep, navy-blue backdrop surrounded by national flags.

A picture can also hammer a thousand nails into the coffin of a campaign far more eloquently than any verbal gaffe or faux pas. Remember the unfortunate yet hugely qualified Democrat nominee in 1988, Governor Michael Dukakis, undone by an apparently innocuous picture of himself in a tank, looking like nothing so much as an errant chipmunk. Or former British Labour leader Ed Miliband's famous awkwardness in front of the camera, whether eating a bacon sandwich, gurning at a bunch of schoolkids or standing in front of his election pledges. One of which resembled nothing so much as a massive political tombstone.

Being spontaneous and the story of the new CEO

We have some considerable experience working in the glorious rainbow nation of South Africa. It's a fascinating country, full of hope. In the mix of massive, unprecedented changes and underlying tensions as well, South Africans are overwhelmingly more optimistic than almost any country in the West. In fact, 55%

told us their lives have improved over the past five years, while even more (63%) say they expect things to get better in the near future.[1] But this is in spite of, not because of, those in power. From a 'trust' perspective, the country's political institutions and politicians find themselves almost universally underwater, while endemic corruption is a top-tier concern for no less than three quarters (75%) of those we questioned.

So how can you possibly hope to communicate and influence effectively in such a hostile atmosphere?

Back in the late 1990s, after taking the 11-hour flight down to South Africa from London, we met the newly appointed CEO at the main Frito-Lay factory in Johannesburg to talk about several major organisational issues that the business was tackling at the time. With no pre-conceived ideas on what he would be like, our first impression was how engaging the guy was; truly passionate about people, not 'process' or 'productivity'.

The first task on arrival? The standard 'walkabout' of the factory, to get a feel of the working environment and to ask some of the workers about how the company communicates with them, and, in this case, the new CEO.

These interactions tell you more in five minutes than a 90-minute 'death by PowerPoint' presentation on the latest employee survey results. In fact, the more you listened, the more you discovered that no one really knew him. And this was in spite of the fact that he had been in his job for over three months. Had he taken a vow of silence?

After the tour, we asked him what he had done to communicate with employees and to start building his own reputation. He was surprised when it was revealed that most of the people questioned didn't even know his name, let alone what he was like as a person or leader. As he put it, "I don't understand as we sent out an organisational announcement on email and put printed copies up in the canteen and staff rest areas."

There it was – 'change management' at its finest.

It's fair to say that Frito-Lay, like most big organisations, was obsessed with sending announcements out. The belief seemed to be 'if I've communicated something – anything – I've done my job'. In fact, every senior appointment was honoured with an organisational announcement that a tiny fraction of the business actually bothered to read: normally the person involved and their direct reports. In South Africa, this wasn't just self-defeating; it was positively destructive, reinforcing the idea of a 'them and us' culture in a country that was supposed to be tearing 'artificial' barriers down. The 'thems' were – or at least appeared to be – totally preoccupied with themselves... not the people they were supposed to be leading.

Following a chat over coffee with the local (and highly charismatic) HR Director – who at the time was one of the few black South Africans on the management team – we soon figured out what was going on. He laughed and said that he had been telling the CEO this for months, but he just didn't get it. He explained that illiteracy is so prevalent in South Africa – and this was particularly so among older persons who were marginalised from educational opportunities under the Apartheid system. At that time, around one in five of the South African population aged 20 years and above in 1998 had never been to school.[2] He pointed out that there are 35 different languages spoken widely in South Africa as well; English, by contrast, is spoken by less than 10% of the population.

So, Frito-Lay in South Africa had a real problem, largely stemming from the fact that they had rather stubbornly not considered their audience. Their announcements were written, beautifully written in some cases, in the Queen's English. They were posted on noticeboards to be read by an audience that – for the most part – couldn't read at all, let alone read English. In short – and this is an especially virulent disease among communications departments the world over, by no means a South African pandemic – this was a classic case of thinking about 'getting the message out' and not about what the audience needs. It's not what you say that counts; it's what they hear.

But the good news from this insight is that it helped us figure out how to change the way the company communicated to employees in the factory. There were all kinds of ancillary benefits. For instance, we knew that the business had suffered from a massive challenge with theft. Not just a few packets of crisps, or several cans of Pepsi here and there, but whole lorry loads of product, AND the lorry as well! Why would this be? Well, as the HR Director explained, someone could steal a lorry, sell the products on board, sell the lorry and sell the container to someone who in turn would then convert it into a house! From a business perspective, this was no great source of mirth. The company was having the equivalent of one lorry a week stolen from the factory backyard.

This huge financial and reputational cost to the business was the catalyst to develop an entirely picture-based language in order to help explain certain things to staff and preach the risks associated with theft. In many ways, it was an early version of emojis.

In total, we had about 20 pictures with key messages; today, the emoji alphabet has 2,823 images to help people communicate without using a single word. It's the perfect example of a picture speaking 1,000 words; or if you prefer the words attributed to Napoleon Bonaparte, "a good sketch is better than a long speech." There are no points for using more language or complexity than your audience needs.

In cities all around the world today, we see street artists use the power of imagery to creatively convey a message. From Banksy's protest images on the subjects of climate change and Brexit, through to the Barack Obama 'Hope' poster designed by artist Shepard Fairey – the iconic representation of his 2008 presidential campaign – good words can change actions and behaviours; but good pictures, visuals and video can incite whole new emotions, empathy and inspiration.

This kind of visual communication is especially potent – for good and ill – in such an ethnically diverse terrain as South Africa. We had to go deeper than simply drawing pictures; our programme created a whole picture book dictionary and got employees who could speak one of the 35 languages to educate their colleagues on what those pictures meant in practice. An engaged audience is far more likely to be an empowered audience – and one that will deliver for you. Our result in South Africa was more prosaic, but for Frito-Lay, highly productive: thefts plummeted, going down by over 60%, while safety improved, and productivity went through the roof.

All from a few innovative pictures that changed the way a business engaged with its diverse workforce, because the old approach was keeping them surreptitiously pinned back. Ask yourself the same question: are you stuck with using the same conventional wisdom when it comes to communicating?

Science is changing conventional wisdom

Neuroscience and behavioural psychology increasingly demonstrate the emotional and instinctive aspects of our minds drive communication. And the latest research illustrates that should you be engaged in trying to change the mind of someone who vehemently disagrees with you, introducing a *fact* into the argument is almost the worst place one can start. But let's not confuse 'facts' with 'reason' and say a few words about using both to establish a context for change.

In any communication, discussion of *context* – i.e. the situation in which you and your audience find yourself today – is the most important aspect you need to get right. It is so important that it should be at least half of your word count or airtime. And yes, the plurality of this should be about matching the mood of your audience. But a fact or three is critical, too. It is the minor note in the melody, the gherkin in the sandwich. But without it, the whole ensemble of your argument would fall apart.

Facts do work best in threes: on its own, a single fact is about as credible as an unsupported assertion and more likely to drive someone away from your point of view. Two could be a simple coincidence. But three facts look like a trend, even to a sceptic. Remember the 'rule of three' if you are genuinely interested in establishing reasons to be believed.

Similarly, do not underestimate the impact of a fact that *surprises* or enlightens your audience. When we are having a conversation with someone, we could be surprising them or boring them. But if you can accomplish the former, you will have an exponential effect on your impact. We like to have our minds surprised or illuminated, and it doesn't take a statistical geek to do it. Ronald Reagan had a gift not only for amusing, avuncular anecdotes but also for inserting the telling, small-but-unprovable detail into them. "They're having to eat rat meat on the Moscow subway", was one that he famously used to tip a hat to the Soviet Union's economic decline.

But beware. Fact junkies often miss this vital lesson we remind our clients of; not all facts are equal. For example, do Australians care more that 63% of indigenous species are threatened by forest degradation or that koalas are predicted to be extinct from the wild within a decade or two? Consider that oh-so-important but easily overlooked two-word question in the minds of your audience: so what? Why should what you are talking about *matter to me*? And what might be the positive consequences (a vital word, both tangibly and emotionally) of what you are proposing?

It is astonishing to us exactly how often clients approach us with clashing – or utterly contradictory – objectives. And so, sorting out your objectives from the story you must tell (and the communications strategy it will encompass) is key to successfully engaging your audiences. There is no value in being quick and nimble if you have no idea of what it is that you are trying to accomplish in the end.

The conventional means of 'public relations' used to be to begin with your message and then figure out how to tell people what they need to know. That may have worked 20 years ago, but not now. Communications today is as much a science as it is an art, and this requires a deeper level of planning and preparation as the digital revolution means that you rarely get more than one chance to get it right. Start by *understanding the context of what is happening around you* because conventional wisdom is very often wrong.

LAW OF NIMBLICITY #3:

ALWAYS LOOK TO YOURSELF BEFORE BLAMING OTHERS

"Of all the talents bestowed upon men, none is so precious as the gift of oratory. He who enjoys it wields a power more durable than that of a great king."

Sir Winston Churchill

While people, politicians and PR departments have always competed for it, the war for *attention* becomes more intense than ever. From airlines to Amnesty International, from big businesses to bipartisan policy groups, clients increasingly find that purely *factual* arguments are less effective in persuasion than *emotive* assertions. For instance, we struggle to visualise what '12.7 million tonnes of plastic' dumped in the ocean looks like. But it takes a heart of stone not to be moved by the plight of an innocent turtle or whale drowned by our thoughtlessly discarded dustbin bags.

This willingness to address our emotions, our subconscious, or our 'gut' can leave our rational mind gasping to keep up. But, echoing Churchill, it is still those who have *mastered the music of emotions* that we follow.

We live in an age of so-called 'alternative facts', but boomer anxieties about the 'post-truth' world are often over-done. Spin is perennial. Facts have always come with points of view. The virtual world is simply more divided than the one that preceded it, so it might be more accurate to think of (strongly) 'competing perspectives'... but that would not generate as many clicks, would it? We are becoming ever more certain about our *uncertainty*. And thus, when it comes to trust, we turn to those *closer* to us. So, this chapter looks at the psychology good leaders use to *empower* their teams and tribes.

Much of what we discuss in this book would have been unthinkable (let alone practicably impossible) before the technological revolution of fifteen or 20 years ago. But infotech hasn't done away with the need for good leaders. Instead, some ancient lessons simply need recasting for the modern era. Old light through new windows. The very *speed* of change today means these principles must evolve into a new communications approach that melds new and innovative approaches, with the timeless approaches to communication that have been honed over thousands of years.

Some things – if they don't actually repeat – certainly seem to rhyme through history. The media may change, but the message stays the same. Slick salesmen sell 'simple, hassle-free solutions' to complex problems. It has always been a quicker dime to be a critic on the sidelines (or firing off pre-scripted zingers) than to strip off and get into the arena yourself. History has always been made by those who show up, and this has not changed. Our work here is directed towards the communicators and change-makers seeking a signal amid the noisy circumstances in which they find themselves.

But among the vast amounts of advice provided by academics and experts, where's the best place to look?

Learning from others

It is a basic human characteristic to seek to model our behaviour on those we admire in our 'tribe'. From how we learn to talk to climbing the career ladder, we are *socialised* beings – learning more from each other than texts or tracts. And so, we turn – in our hundreds of thousands – to the people we want to emulate when it comes to being a better version of our natural self: elite athletes, coaches, yogis, philosophers, military heroes. The 'winning edge'; efficiency and effectiveness; mindfulness and meditation. Every week, it seems, someone else has a new 'five-point plan' to sell us success and serenity.

In terms of communication, we have found insight from the military expertise of the SAS in the UK and the Seals in the US to be uniquely helpful. Although it may seem a long way from your work at a charity or company, the military's approach – distilled down to its essentials – can teach us a lot, even if our work is not a matter of life or death. Britain's Ant Middleton and ex-US Navy Seal Jocko Willink are just two former military leaders who are examples of the 'latest' thinking, which, in fact, like many of the newest lessons we learn, is founded on very old concepts indeed.

When a military leader walks into a debrief and blames everyone else for something that has gone wrong on the battlefield, that attitude pervades the entire team. Defensiveness invites attack. Leaders who blame their subordinates are tacitly blaming themselves because it is the leader's job to equip their team for victory... or at least, it is meant to be. Courageous leadership means *ownership*, right down through the chain of command. There are no 'bad teams' – only bad leaders.

While this may not always be possible in an organisation or campaign of many thousands, the thought is one we'd endorse: if your communication or campaign isn't functioning as you believe it should, first look to *yourself*. Is there a better, more clear and concise way that you can convey your plans? This applies up the 'chain of command', as well as downwards. Have you involved your subordinates in the decisions you've taken? Good leaders have nothing to fear from well-articulated questions or concerns; in fact, they should seek them out.

Establishing listening, preparation time and research into your communication planning is one of the most powerful changes you can make. There was a time when PRs and publicist types would claim to have a 'black box' of tricks that could 'guarantee' communications success. Not anymore. As advanced analytics have revolutionised politics, Opta statistics have transformed football worldwide. They tell a coach everything from the distance ran by a player in a match to pass completion percentages. There is no reason for you *not* to know precisely how your team is thinking and feeling at any given moment.

In the 2020s, the evidence is always 'on the field' in the form of employee surveys, instant-response dials (for message-testing) or analysis of audience comments. Some still shy away from this 'Moneyball' reality, but it is wise not to be one of them. Yes, data is just data – it is only useful as part of a larger, more coherent approach. But recognise that we are all much more *accountable* today for our communication, incoming and outward. So, use that data as a vital means of taking responsibility and *listening.*

Of course, good listening is a fundamental, key skill that anybody can learn – but it takes real *will* to enact.

Empowering activists

Amnesty International is one of the world's largest, longest established and most venerable human rights campaigning organisations. Founded over 60 years ago, Amnesty has an enviable track record of success, involving some seven million members in fighting human rights abuses no matter where they occur in the world. However, that longevity also had its downside in that AI's organisational structures were largely of a bygone age. Myriad committees and multiple layers reflected organisations like the United Nations rather than the way activists campaign in 2021. In order to enable real responsibility, Amnesty needed to evolve.

"It was really a question of giving activists the opportunity to step up and lead for themselves," says Amanda Atlee, one of Amnesty's leading organisers for over a decade and a passionate, genuine advocate for human rights. "Previously, two staff members would support dozens of groups across New South Wales, say… and activists were really dependent on them, and they had a radically different level and quality of experience as a result." Rather than being *directed* by some remote figure in 'HQ', Amnesty wanted to embrace the idea of activists *owning* the campaigns they fought.

The change has not been without its challenges. As Atlee points out, it is actually surprising how many of us actually don't *want* to lead! In addition, there was cynicism from those who simply saw the exercise as a cost-cutting measure (which it was, in part). However, where it worked, and Amnesty volunteers *bought into* the new approach, some of the results were astounding. "In one group, we had an activist draw up a detailed, 20-page strategy for local recruitment and campaigns that was *far* better than any of us could have come up with," Atlee says. "All they needed us for was some feedback and to sign off on it."

There are numerous other specific examples of Amnesty activists being able to take ownership and *agency* in a way the old model simply didn't allow. Whereas previously, the organisation had been somewhat transfixed by membership numbers – in the way that some are with 'clicks' or 'likes' – this had changed. Amnesty realised that it was worth *far* more to have a dozen engaged and *empowered* local members than hundreds who did nothing more than simply show up on a database.

It hasn't all gone smoothly. Cultural change can take a while in a successful NGO that has lasted *generations*. But Amnesty simply illustrates a broader cultural shift towards the kind of 'extreme ownership' that Jocko Willink writes about. Campaigns *depend* on volunteers and activists taking ownership. And so modern campaigning organisations – whether 'XR' or Airbnb's 'user-generated content' – need to *empower* their movements while leaders retain *accountability* for their ultimate success or failure. The way we engage is changing. Before you blame others... look to yourself.

The simple truth of ancient hatreds: Iraq and Zimbabwe

The British-US writer Christopher Hitchens once claimed, "A man's life is incomplete until he has tasted love, poverty and war." As relatively well-padded consultants, we can nonetheless claim to have experienced the first two ingredients.

The third is harder to come by and yet remains a vital experience. Iraq in 2009–2010 was a country backsliding towards increased violence and sectarianism. The hope that, perhaps, the US-led coalition's 'liberation' of the country could lead to a thriving, multi-ethnic democracy in the middle of the Middle East was fading. It wasn't only The Hitch who was forced to reconsider his earlier optimism.

Our party formed part of Ayad Allawi's Iraqiya coalition (or list) and was the group most committed to a fully secular Iraq, not determined by allegiance to sect or faction. Allawi himself was, and is, a hugely courageous figure who had survived at least three direct assassination attempts and was rumoured to have shot several terrorists personally. The party leadership was determined to bring the latest campaign techniques to the region's newest democracy, to be data-driven. We applied deep opinion research to Iraq's 19 governorates (provinces), matching our promises and prose to the priorities of Iraqi citizens. Our message was driven by the hope of unity after Saddam's dictatorship and years of internecine struggle. No, it wasn't revolutionary stuff… unless you were Iraqi, of course.

Headquartered in one of Uday Hussein's former palaces on the banks of the Tigris, it was possible to sense the growing tension in the night air of Baghdad. One evening we went out into the garden, and one of us made the mistake of climbing up into one of the guard towers. It was mere seconds before we heard the sound of gunfire.

The real heroes of the campaign were the foot soldiers. 'Door-knocking' in the suburbs of some anonymous town is a staple of any Western campaign. It took on a different meaning in a country struggling to stand alone, riven by suspicion and animosity between Sunni and Shi'a, ex-Ba'athists and not, members of rival militias and mosques. At one point, we lost two volunteers, killed in cold blood, and thought, 'we can't carry on'. The Iraqis begged us not to stop campaigning.

As it became clear how competitive the race was, it became equally clear that Maliki's State of Law campaign would leave no stone un-thrown in the battle for victory. Far from a message of unity and togetherness, they focused on the ancient grievances of the Shi'a majority — persecuted for so long under Saddam by Iraq's Sunnis (who numbered some six million fewer). Campaign videos emerged showing the slaughter of the Shi'a (including dead bodies and all)… the message could hardly have been clearer or more calculated.

In the end, 62% of brave Iraqis came out to vote in spite of the violence and vile rhetoric. Iraqiya also emerged as marginally the victor, winning the largest share of the vote and two more seats than Maliki. However, the sitting Prime Minister used all the advantages of incumbency to make it clear that he would not be going quietly.

Emma Sky was the political adviser to the US forces in Iraq at the time. Her contemporaneous account makes fascinating reading for anyone interested in the story of post-invasion Iraq:

> *"When we asked Maliki about his retirement plans, it was immediately obvious that Maliki was not contemplating stepping down. He claimed a massive election fraud and that the Mujahideen al-Khalq (an Iranian opposition group) had used satellites to change the results in the computer. This was despite the computers being stand-alone, not attached to the internet and with thousands of independent election observers. His advisers were telling him that he would win big, with a majority of over a hundred seats. He demanded a full recount. Maliki was becoming scary."*[3]

Indeed, he was, and having lost the election, Nouri Al-Maliki managed to preside over a further four years of increasingly sectarian rule as Iraq slid towards increasing conflict between ISIS, the US and innumerable home-grown factions.

It was a similar story two years before, in 2008. Zimbabwe's long-term dictator Robert Mugabe had insufficiently 'fixed' that country's parliamentary and presidential elections of that spring. Rather embarrassingly, the 80-something-year-old tyrant found himself in a run-off with the Movement for Democratic Change, led by courageous stalwart Morgan Tsvangirai. Sensing that, after *decades* of misrule in the one-time 'breadbasket of Southern Africa', Mugabe's time might, at last, be up, resources and help started to flood into the MDC.

A campaign team was assembled in Johannesburg, comprising some of the smartest operatives from around the globe to help. Australia's Lynton Crosby, later to mastermind David Cameron's surprise British general election win in 2015[4], was accompanied by his partner, the genial and streetwise Mark Fullbrook. From the States, Paul Blank and taciturn genius Joe Trippi were recruited, the latter renowned for having managed 'Dean for America' in 2004 (as well as being rumoured to be the model for Toby Ziegler's character in *The West Wing*). In so doing, Trippi came up with the original blueprint – not to mention many of the staff – for Obama's historic win four years later. This would truly be a heavyweight effort.

While the MDC's hugely impressive electoral 'ground game' continued throughout Zimbabwe, the team focused on the critical international aspect. With the world now looking on, would Mugabe be forced to allow a relatively free and fair vote? The campaign ramped up the pressure on multinational companies, including Tesco, not to do business with Mugabe. Meanwhile, Trippi's online expertise was deployed to keep Zimbabwe on US screens, while even printers De La Rue were successfully pressured to stop printing Mugabe's worthless banknotes.

The early days of the run-off campaign proceeded relatively normally until it became clear that the very real prospect was an outright MDC victory. At that point, Mugabe sent in the goons. What began as a raid on the MDC's headquarters spread out onto the streets as innocent bystanders were arrested or beaten by alcohol-fuelled thugs armed with crowbars.

In our headquarters, one of the author's found himself tied up at gunpoint sometime after four in the morning by three large and over-enthusiastic 'door knockers' demanding to be given 'the computers'. It was an hour or two before he could be untied by a sleeping (and half-naked) Joe Trippi. A disbelieving Lynton Crosby could only ask, "Fair dinkum?!?" when he was told the story later that morning.

Ultimately, Tsvangirai was forced to pull out of the run-off to avoid a mass loss of life. Mugabe got away with it because he knew no country would intervene to displace him from office. Furthermore, he could still draw on some cachet as 'the man who stuck it to the white guys' in Southern Africa. Tragically and almost comically, he was able to rule for a further nine years. Hyperinflation hit 79.6 billion per cent five months after the 'vote', and his country fell further into the quicksand of poverty as the ruthless – and increasingly senseless – dictator clung stubbornly to power.

Neither campaign, in Iraq or Zimbabwe, can be credited as a 'win' or necessarily even a success. However, each was hugely worthwhile and demonstrated the profound importance of the ties of blood and brotherhood. We underestimate them at our peril. Ultimately, the tools of our democratic trade were found pathetically wanting in the face of brute force. Each case demonstrated the *limits* to which we could 'own the outcome', even as we took responsibility for our team. In one, we were lucky to escape with our lives.

Leveraging your strengths

While Sir Christopher Gent was the darling of the Stock Exchange and the public face of Vodafone's incredible and rapid growth through acquisition, it was his deputy Sir Julian Horn-Smith who was the unsung hero.

As deputy CEO and chief operating officer at Vodafone, Julian was responsible for acquisitions and became well known as the chief dealmaker, ensuring that the multi-billion-dollar acquisitions of national telecommunication companies would seamlessly work together. It was Julian who took it upon himself to ensure that the sum of the Vodafone parts would be greater than the whole.

His tough, straight-talking, no-B.S. style became legendary across the organisation, with employees at all levels both in awe and in fear of his presence. But he was no authoritarian, taking extreme care to *listen* to what his team was telling him – and taking full responsibility when things went wrong.

Underneath Horn-Smith's gruff exterior was a leader who cared deeply for the business and the people. And it is *this* trait that we find in common with effective principles, whether in business or politics. When you really care, it shows. And it becomes that much harder to pass the buck elsewhere.

In 2001, Vodafone launched a new set of company values called the 'four passions' for results, customers, the environment and their employees. These were designed to bring together the very best of the local business cultures and start developing a 'One Vodafone' mindset across the group.

To demonstrate the values in action, Chris and Julian embarked on a whirlwind world tour to visit all 16 operating companies (countries) and talk in person to local employees about Vodafone's strategy, its values and future ambition. From New Zealand to Egypt, the reception they received surprised them. Employees genuinely bought into the strategy – and appreciated the fact that the business' group chief executive had travelled so far to discuss it with them.

After the dust had settled on the final country visit, like a couple of enthused teenagers returning home from a year of backpacking, Chris and Julian were already planning their next programme of country visits.

There was, as ever, a fly in the ointment. As we listened to our local colleagues' feedback on the sessions, it became apparent that while Sir Christopher had star billing and people were thrilled to hear from the group chief executive, the jury was out on Julian.

Words such as 'dull' and 'uninspiring' emerged when discussing Horn-Smith's town hall presentations. It soon became clear that the 'Chris and Julian' show was not the compelling double bill that we had first imagined.

Conversely, the feedback on Julian's more intimate conversations with small groups of local leaders and high-potential employees couldn't have been more different. Sentiments such as 'charismatic', 'engaging' and 'personable' emerged and provided an insight into the communications style that best suited the deputy chief executive and chief operating officer. Change the *context*, and the insipid communicator became *inspired*.

When Julian received this feedback, he sat back in his chair to a *highly* audible silence. Known for something of a volcanic temper, his immediate subordinates expected him to explode as if he had just had Christmas cancelled. But he didn't, instead, retreating into a deep reflective silence. Eventually – and totally calmly – he intoned, "it's not about what I think I should do; it's about doing what is right for our local leaders and their employees." In other words, communication serves his *audience*, not himself.

The following year, Chris and Julian did another series of visits to the Vodafone operating companies, and this time, they played to their strengths. While Chris did the town hall 'keynote' presentations to large groups of employees, Julian spent quality time having facilitated and more informal conversations with local leaders.

Later, he privately admitted that he never particularly *enjoyed* making formal presentations to large groups. They always felt stilted and phoney. Instead, he felt more comfortable when he could be his more authentic self – unscripted and having a simple, *real* conversation.

A great example of Nimblicity in practice by a leader who had the humility to know when he should change his approach to serve the wider purpose of the business.

LAW OF NIMBLICITY #4:

HARNESSING TECHNOLOGY IS ESSENTIAL, NOT A NICE-TO-HAVE

"Once every five to seven years, a company emerges that changes not just the technology industry, but the world... In 2011, Twitter broke through into the elite group of companies that profoundly shape our world."

Peter Fenton

We shape technology; thereafter, it shapes us. Just as the printing press took the word of God from a few hundred pious monks and placed it in the hands of people everywhere, television took the *aural* platform of radio and made it visual. The result isn't just a change of communication — it is a change of *consciousness*. Our whole relationship with those in charge is transformed. Never could public figures not afford to be 'camera ready' again.

A mere decade and a half since Twitter and Facebook connected the world's exploding population – there are 1.8 billion more of us than at the turn of the century – we are living through another of these unheralded upheavals. The *democratisation* of the internet has made 'celebrities' of us (if we so wish) with brands, bodies and 'influencer' status to match. This chapter looks at the transformation this has wrought in how we campaign and communicate – whether we like it or not.

The rewiring of the modern media mind

In 1961, then newly appointed Federal Communications Commission (FCC) chairman Newton Minow gave a now-legendary speech, warning of the pernicious impact of the brand-new communications medium, television. "I urge each of you to sit down in front of your television and stay there for a day," he fumed. "I can assure you that what you will observe is a vast wasteland."

Minow was far from alone in worrying about the rising dominance of frivolity and 'fun-based programming'. This took the place of the more austere, considered and contemplative world of radio, books and newspapers. The concern wasn't just for the standard of discourse but about our whole level of *morality.* Please stop us if any of this is starting to sound eerily similar to complaints about the ubiquity of cat GIFs on our kids' tablets.

Others reacted differently. For instance, the producers of *Gilligan's Island* – an absolute masterpiece of 1960s frivolity, if ever there was one – named the show's boat the SS *Minnow* in their fulminating critic's honour. Whether full of wonder or fulminating, *everybody* recognised that the world has changed. As Richard Nixon noted, having famously been undone by the new medium during the first televised US presidential debate, "It's all that counts now – how you come across on the Tube."

The trivialisation of TV debates and their consequences for our ability to weigh difficult topics continues today. "God only knows what social media is doing to children's brains," says Sean Parker – one of Facebook's founding fathers. It is no longer a question of if these changes are happening – only how. But just as television created the petri dish of the current epidemics of sedentary obesity and 'reality TV' emptiness, is that the whole story? Would, for instance, the Eastern Bloc have thrown off the rusty shackles of communism without the televisual demonstration of the West's superior standard of living?

Driven by the need for revenue, journalism gives way to 'click bait' competition, shamelessly playing on our need for dopamine – or rage – in equal measure. 'Coffee Can Kill You!' or 'Cute Panda Cubs!' Our language has changed to create a greater informality (and thus, a shared sense of belonging) than ever before. But this, too, easily curdles into community's twisted stepsister, tribalism. It is not for nothing that 'Web 5.0' is already being called the *emotional* web.

Our present interconnectedness puts the Ukrainian activist in the same virtual room as the US gamer. By its very nature, it becomes more and more difficult for the powerful, prosperous few to live on an island of wealth in a sea of want. The Arab Spring was as much a product of the modern communications revolution as its televisual predecessor helped instigate the uprising within the old Warsaw Pact countries. Twitter, Facebook, Instagram and the rest shone a light on the face of the ancient regimes of the East, and it became clear that the young didn't enjoy the vision of their future that they saw.

Some ask whether social media enables the rise of a kind of 'new tyranny', where evil Russian 'bots' hack elections, exert influence and subvert democracy in the West. Having fought in many of those elections and campaigns believed to have been subverted by the hackers, we find their influence to be real but hugely over stated. Russia's economy, for example, is smaller than that of Spain. 'Tweet farms' and trolls are undoubtedly real, but they are not the true explanations of Donald Trump, populism more generally or Brexit. The undercurrents of unfairness and dissatisfaction with political 'elites' were detectable long before the earthquakes of 2016. Proper rules and regulations should do much to dispel the conspiracy theories surrounding social media. After all, haven't we long insisted on the same for our broadcast media?

Closer, closer and closer

Ultimately, technology has increased the perceived closeness between 'leader' and 'follower'. At the same time, the role of **emotion** and **empathy** (i.e. not 'understanding', but an emotional connection) has dramatically increased. We have become more emotionally intelligent in how we – as an audience – interpret what our leaders are telling us. We expect them to be able to communicate across a broader range of emotions, and our senses are more attuned to a wider emotive vocabulary than ever before.

Consider the following from President Franklin Roosevelt's second 'fireside chat', delivered in the springtime of 1933 and a masterpiece of the time of leadership communication:

> *"On a Sunday night a week after my inauguration I used the radio to tell you about the banking crisis and the measures we were taking to meet it. I think that in that way I made clear to the country various factors that might otherwise have been misunderstood and in general provided a means of understanding which did much to restore confidence. Tonight, eight weeks later, I come for the second time to give you my report – in the same spirit and by the same means to tell you about what we have been doing and what we are planning to do."*

In the 30s, this kind of 'intimacy' – the President addressing the nation 'one to one' was considered almost unbelievably interpersonal in nature. Read the passage again. And imagine now if this same passage were delivered by President Biden – who makes no secret of his desire to emulate FDR himself – today. Note the differences in syntax, adjectival use and formality, and Roosevelt seems hopelessly stilted and stiff.

Next, let's turn the clock 'four score years' forwards to 2016 and President Obama's remarks upon introducing various executive orders to limit access to guns, following the latest spate of high school shootings in the States:

> *"Think about what happened three weeks ago. Zaevion Dobson was a sophomore at Fulton High School in Knoxville, Tennessee. He played football; beloved by his classmates and his teachers. The week before Christmas, he headed to a friend's house to play video games.*

> *"He wasn't in the wrong place at the wrong time. He hadn't made a bad decision. He was exactly where any other kid would be. Your kid. My kids. And then gunmen started firing. And Zaevion – who was in high school, hadn't even gotten started in life – dove on top of three girls to shield them from the bullets.*

> *"And he was shot in the head. And the girls were spared. He gave his life to save theirs – an act of heroism a lot bigger than anything we should ever expect from a 15-year-old."*

The informality of his approach. The naming of a specific person in a specific town gives the President's remarks enormous tangibility. While the use of "kid… your kid… my kids" does more than any policy or pronouncement could do to establish a link between the chief and his tribe. Once, we were unashamed to be 'talked down to'. Today, it's unthinkable. And, if further proof were needed, remember too that President Obama both broke down in tears delivering these remarks – only months after publicly (and almost spontaneously) *bursting into song*… it is impossible to picture FDR – or the other leaders we lionise from the Second World War – doing the same.

As we have argued, the internet – in its latest form – is a supremely *democratising* force. We consider ourselves 'on the same level' as our chiefs and C-suites. Deference is dead. We demand to know more of how they think and feel, as much as what they will do. Even though we find the simplistic bluster, boasting and braggadocio of many populists coarse, we forgive it if we believe it to be 'authentic'.

We are seemingly more forgiving of our leaders' foibles – whether linguistic gaffes, sexual misadventures or the follies of youth – when we can see *ourselves* in that picture. By contrast, when that flaw is something alien and appalling (a racial slur, perhaps), the internet ensures that it cannot 'be disappeared' by a willing lackey. Retribution and reprimand are swift today, and brutal. As (our own famously gloomy) 'Generation X' and the (more cheerful, if more broke) millennials move into the prime of their lives, this trend is only likely to increase.

The convergence of aspiration

Technology has also had a profound impact on the 'A' component of ORACLE: aspiration. It has created a window on a world, previously bricked up and barricaded off. From Buckingham Palace to Belorussia, via Beverly Hills, it has *broadened* and *flattened* our perspective. Simultaneously, it has opened our eyes to what might be possible. People from the slums of Mumbai to the favelas of Rio can now see what others have… and that inevitably invites comparison.

Meanwhile, we know from polling that the percentage of people agreeing that 'their children will have it better than they do' is gradually eroding across Europe and the States. The world's flattening and interconnectedness have affected our sense of 'our place in the world' – and our power to change it. Just as we feast our eyes on a limitless buffet, we find ourselves further and further removed from its bounty. So, our aspirations aren't opposed to the increasing *anxieties* that we feel… instead, they march together in lockstep.

People have turned, in varying degrees of anger, to politicians and business leaders, only to find that their answers are limited – or Luddite in nature. The greater the clamour for more 'controls' on immigration… internet transparency… or tax dodging… the more we glimpse our leaders' impotence. In some respects, populists resemble the *saboteurs* of the First Industrial Revolution, smashing machinery up with their wooden shoes.[5] This is simply the rage of the impotent against the inevitable. And it persists in the Fourth Industrial Revolution we inhabit today.

More than having a window into the lives of 'the other', we can now open a direct dialogue with them as well. It can be no surprise that judgments – on both sides – swiftly follow. US Treasury Secretary Steven Mnuchin's (multi-millionaire) wife found herself drawn into a social media row with a taxpayer who objected to her use of a private jet. The fracas 'went viral' because it exposed the fault lines of 'status anxiety' and the legitimate aspirations of those whom the government is, nominally at least, supposed to serve.

If it is unacceptable for Africans to live 'in a sea of poverty, surrounded by islands of plenty'… then surely it must be so in Appalachia or Aberdeen? As our borders are slowly stripped away, so is our sense of safety and security. This leads to both increasing resentments… and diminishing self-esteem and self-worth. While a premium is placed upon commanders and communicators who sound like us and *put us in the centre of the picture.*

Technology doesn't just shorten our attention span while dividing our brains with a dizzying array of options... it changes our consciousness, too. The things we hope for and aspire to are simply of a different order to that of only a few decades ago. Our institutions – from venerable educational ivory towers... to Amnesty International – struggle to keep up. In order to properly comprehend the changing world around us, we need to have a proper handle on the new ways in which we express our desires, dreams and *aspirations*.

Meanwhile, we are all 'content producers' now – 'mass media' replaced by peer-to-peer production, our aspirations converging on one another.

Reputations on the run

Many of the effects are being played out before our eyes. The ability to order anything from a robot to reading material and have it arrive within 24 hours may be 'peak consumerism' (so long as we don't ask too many questions about how some of those eye-catching efficiencies are accomplished). More insidious still is the culture of childish lawlessness that the internet enables. Its borderless world has no equivalent police force.

Some welcome the 'end of secrecy' promised by the likes of WikiLeaks, but does secrecy really have *no* uses? Should we all be able to publish anything we want – in the name of 'getting it ALL out there' and damn the consequences? Welcome to the world of the internet pile-on, and never let the facts get in the way of a good story.

Whether #MeToo, #BlackLivesMatter or the hapless (and previously seemingly untouchable) Ellen DeGeneres, there is nothing quite like the sight of a reputation being irretrievably shredded in mere seconds. And nothing, apart from our appetite for blood being sated, to bring one to a halt.

The 'traditional' news media always included some recourse to factual inaccuracies, innuendoes or downright lies being written about you – whether 'Letters to the Editor', say, or the independent Press Complaints Commission, or even *The Guardian*'s infamous (and often hilarious) 'Corrections and Clarifications' page – there was at least a lifeline. The online world offers no such respite.

We have already seen something of how capable our chimp brains are of rationally sifting through data to draw rigorous, logical conclusions. With *trillions* of posts now being published every month, it becomes impossible to police (least of all by the tech giants, as caught-out and ill-equipped as the rest of us). In conflict online as on the battlefield, truth is always the first casualty of war. *Plus ça change…*

Adolescent anxieties

In some of our recent (US) research, 48% of people told us that they could not find $400 should they need it for an emergency. Which means they are pushed into the clutches of high-interest lenders or credit card companies – two industries that blossom with every passing financial catastrophe. At the same time, we're encouraged to be more *aspirational* than at any point in history.

Our social media feeds are deluged with photoshopped images of impossibly gorgeous and gluttonous 'friends' or 'followers' (and what a revealing word *that* is). Our culture teaches the idea that we can 'have it all' – the partner, the career, the lifestyle – if only we *want* it enough. And that sits alongside the idea that if you don't… well, it's your fault. After all, the world is flat, isn't it?

This grim logic has caused chronic *status anxiety*, especially among men and younger women – two groups among whom depression-related illness has spread – to far exceed the number of people ultimately likely to be claimed by COVID-19. In our own face-to-face research, respondents freely admit the desperation caused by apparently unlimited options and opportunity.

For instance, a young singleton in 2022 has sight of more potential mates (of whatever gender) in a few minutes of swiping left than their great-grandfather had in decades of life spent in his hometown or village. This colossal increase in the realm of what we're exposed to hides the less palatable truth that increasing numbers of men are not 'mating' at all… driven out of the dating pool by perceived lack of status. Every year, the number of 'eligible' (i.e. educated, well-resourced) single males drops in comparison to their rising female counterparts. It is small wonder that the leading cause of death for men under the age of 45 now – in most Western societies – is no longer heart disease or cancer, but suicide.

Among girls a generation younger, the picture is even more stark. NYU Professor Jonathan Haidt has written movingly about the rocketing incidents of depressive episodes and self-harm amid the 'social media generation' (those girls who came of age between 2008 and 2012). He disproves the idea that this is simply because we have 'de-stigmatised' mental illness, or simply improved reporting data. Rates of self-harm have nearly tripled since the advent of social media. And the condition really mushroomed around 2011/12, when access to social media (via smartphones) became more ubiquitous, especially among girls.

> *"The nature of girls' bullying is super-charged by the way social media works… We have impossible beauty standards which allow social comparison like never before… Teenage girls now are at a higher risk of a mental disorder, anxiety or of ending up in hospital because of self-harm."*[6]

Imagine you are one of these 12- or 13-year-old schoolgirls. Comparing yourself to the impossibly perfect likenesses of their 'friends' (another concept that has been surreptitiously redefined since the days of their parents). They feel the need to be 'connected' and spend their time literally rating and commenting on one another as a way of life.

As that noted influencer Plato pointed out, humans are innately 'a social animal… Society precedes the individual'. Our actions, behaviours and speech are *copied* and inculcated – not picked up from a book. We learn from watching one another. So, we are heavily dependent on the respect/attention/love of our peer group – no matter the bloodless souls who tell us that we should be perfectly content with ourselves.

There are deeply ingrained – and scientifically demonstrable – reasons why 1950s 'rebels' all wore identical pompadours… and why people now line up around the block to cover their bodies with tribal tattoos in order to declaim their own specific 'individuality'. Technology dangles the carrot that, somehow, we will be *better able to belong*.

We don't yet fully understand what these new tools are doing to our minds. Many insiders and whistle-blowers have pointed out, 'likes weren't just an add-on to Instagram, Facebook and the rest… they were *fundamental* to social media companies turning a profit'. The 'like' or 'heart' buttons give you a serotonin 'hit' to keep you coming back ('gamification', as it's known in Napa). For instance, Facebook likes are 'stored up' in order that you log on one day and get an increased 'dose'. And that works, whether your goal is telemarketing or terror. ISIS' rise owed as much to Twitter as it did the tactics of Taylor Swift.

Many of social media's founding fathers (and they were mostly men) now have extreme concerns, acknowledging they didn't realise the damage they were doing to our fragile, internal 'wiring'. We have thus created an age that mixes the virtue (or virtue signalling, depending on your point of view) of #ExtinctionRebellion and #TimesUp… alongside the vice of extreme *vanity*.

We have never before allowed our children to be so brutally, straightforwardly sexualised – 'hardcore gender signalling' – and at the same time, immediately gratified by impossible ideas of what 'should' be natural. Is 'success' the development of our character discipline… or attracting thumbs ups by the thousand? The incentives are certainly not evenly weighted. But it is beyond the purpose of this book to seek to remedy all these problems; rather, to set out the dramatically altered *context* in which we find ourselves… and what responsible communicators can learn about this ever-evolving landscape. Technology has truly changed the game.

Taming the online badlands

Social media has placed us into a massive electronic social experiment. It is fair to acknowledge that the tech companies which now dominate our daily lives never expected to find themselves in this deep. Indeed, 'regulation' (which many tech giants now accept as both necessary and/or inevitable) may well ultimately see Google, Facebook and several others broken-up, as they have effectively monopolised connectivity.

We have worked with many of the biggest tech firms in attempting to navigate this terrain. So, this section incorporates lessons we have picked up from Facebook, Google, Airbnb, Microsoft and others we have worked with. Each necessarily views 'issues' through the lens of its own perspective, but perhaps Facebook's is the most all-encompassing – well over half the British population (and fully seven out of ten Americans) use the platform every day.

We found ourselves researching the immediate response of British audiences in the immediate aftermath of the 2017 terrorist atrocity in Manchester – dramatically highlighting the problems of extremist views, violent content, hate speech, teen bullying and freedom-of-speech/'filter bubble' concerns. Facebook found themselves hauled before parliament and struggling to respond to an angry and frightened British public.

The company had already paid a heavy price for describing Russian-backed 'fake news' election-meddling as 'a crazy idea'. In managing frontline campaigns, we have experienced, firsthand, the efforts of foreign 'web brigades' in several national votes. While the influence of Russian (or Saudi) troll farms has been hugely overstated, they nonetheless illustrate how easy it is – on a site with literally trillions of posts – to publish false or misleading content. Simply put, nobody believed that adequate controls were in place. Equally, people were highly aware of their own human tendency to listen overwhelmingly to people and sources they agreed with... so, imposing a kind of 'filter bubble' on themselves, even before the power of the algorithm kicked in.

Interestingly, our digital dial research showed that ordinary people felt that the political focus on 'more regulation' is largely misguided. Bluntly, they questioned whether the government was remotely capable of policing the traffic on Facebook. Footage of Mark Zuckerberg's icy testimony on Capitol Hill to a group of NYU students drew guffaws, not so much from the Facebook founder's awkward and robotic delivery so much as congressmen's child-like questions. "I started receiving advertisements for chocolate... What if I don't want to receive those commercial advertisements?" asked one, who might as well have been asking Zuckerberg for advice on tuning his VCR.

At least, the shared confusion in the face of such vast and varied problems was made abundantly clear. Far clearer than what we should do about them.

For British audiences at least, 'transparency' and 'control' were the watchwords they wanted to see (perhaps not surprisingly, coming less than a year after the 'Brexit' vote). "You just can't regulate everything," as one middle-aged lady put it. Equally, they were uncomfortable with a technological 'fix' – i.e. some kind of algorithm or artificial intelligence determining what is and isn't 'acceptable'. These ordinary people understood instinctively what it took Harvard intellectuals decades to work out; we have all kinds of biases and 'associations' – eliminating them all automatically would be neither possible nor desirable. And on some deeper level, we're reassured by the thought that there is a human being making those kinds of judgment calls.

Governments, again, find themselves trying to police the ever-shifting boundary where one group's right to protest gay marriage becomes 'hate speech' and it is necessary to shut down free religious expression. Average Facebook users responded enthusiastically to the idea of human 'content moderators' working hand in (electronic) glove with artificial intelligence, precisely because we don't altogether trust the idea of a computer ruling what can and cannot be judged 'legitimate' speech.

In the end, our research found that what people wanted was something almost quaintly old-fashioned, which they had taken for granted: mutually agreed rules of the road, which ensured that whatever they – and particularly their children – saw was controlled in some way. 'Free speech' was never meant to mean a free-for-all. It is a crime to scream 'fire' in a crowded theatre – for reasons that we *all* understand.

Realism and *achievability* matter. For instance, no Facebook users we interviewed believed that the site's self-administered age restriction could be credibly maintained. Users tend to see things through a more common-sense lens, "you should be allowed to say whatever you like, but you should not be allowed to incite violence," in the words of one man. If there was one word that summed up what they wanted to hear from the companies that created and profited so handsomely from the tech boom, it was this: *accountability*.

The revolution of the gatekeepers

For decades, the news media – its editors, blowhards and hacks – controlled the power of information flow. 'Media' itself is literally derived from the Latin for 'go-between' (and not, as some scurrilous types have suggested, just the plural of 'mediocrity'). Now, we can go straight to source, and traditional 'news' has lost much of its currency and credibility. But, because we have become 'decentralised', not to mention 'de-televised', does that mean that all restraint and restriction is lost too? Not according to the vast majority.

The idea that social media pages exist simply as a 'platform' – a kind of soapbox which anyone can bestride and for which no one is, therefore, responsible – will not wash. People love social media sites for bringing them together. At the same time, they are anxious about a communications space without borders, boundaries or laws. Freedom is nothing without discipline. And free speech depends on controls, just as free enterprise depends on regulation and taxation to thrive.

Its users wanted – *demanded* – to see that Facebook recognised and respected the community it serves. A business whose stated purpose is to 'give people the power to build community and bring the world closer together' could hardly ignore this, could it?

As a result of this work, Facebook did introduce sweeping changes. High-profile bans on 'white nationalist' and Islamo-fascist organisations were imposed in an inferno of publicity. Facebook-ers were handed more control over what data and materials could be handed over to third parties through their 'privacy settings'. While more quietly – but perhaps more importantly – the algorithm for users' 'newsfeeds' was updated, meaning that people would see more content they might disagree with. The parameters of how much of this we will tolerate are still in their very earliest days, and they will surely evolve again.

Companies like Twitter, Airbnb and Google have a *golden* opportunity to remember that first ideal. To inculcate *peer-to-peer* dialogue… not simply to pulverise one another. Learning from our failures and listening to one another is – in the end – the only hope we have of truly mutually beneficial progress. And now, with the countless channels that technology has provided us, we have the opportunity not just to transform 'communication' but consciousness. Not for the first time, technology has transformed the game.

LAW OF NIMBLICITY #5:

PLANNING AND DELIVERY IS A CONSTANT EVOLUTION, NOT A ONE-OFF EVENT

"Planning is everything; plans are nothing."

Field Marshal Helmuth von Moltke

From all the campaigns we have worked on – internally and externally – the key change brought by new technology and the latest digital revolution has been *immediacy*. Whether change management in big Western bureaucracies or campaigning for girls' education in Pakistan, each generation is born with the expectation of greater speed than the last. Therefore, the agility or responsiveness vector of Nimblicity is so important; in the past, you used to have days to get your message across. Now – thanks to the technological pace of change – you have *seconds*.

The Six-Second Sensation

Six seconds, to be precise (although the number is shrinking all the time). If it's an online video, you have just a few seconds to sink your hooks into their attention or lose it forever. If it is a banner headline, you've got six seconds (or, let's say, a maximum of six words) to captivate them. If it's a radio commercial, you've got the first six seconds before they change the station. And if it's an email, expect it to be ruthlessly deleted if you haven't caught the reader's attention in the opening six words of the subject line.

All it needs is one memorable word with one powerful image for someone to be drawn in. Marketeers understand this and recognise that they can convey a story and evoke audiences by projecting 180 pictures – the number of frames that make up a six-second video.

It is an ever-shrinking audience who will patiently wait for you to finish what you have to say. We may miss them, but we must see the world as it is, not as we might wish it to be. Nearly half of the global population – almost four billion people – are now active social media users using platforms like Twitter, Snapchat, Instagram and TikTok. In many countries, Facebook is *the* primary news source for citizens. And they are all looking for what we would call the 'Six-Second Sensation'; namely, quick, engaging and easily understood content.

And it's not just a Generation-Z thing. With annual user growth of around 10%, it won't be long before even the most die hard technology Luddites will succumb to this. The genie is well and truly out of the bottle, and there is no going back.

Interestingly, however, the other fast-rising trend in podcasts and social media is long-form. With unlimited channels to choose from, people actually enjoy longer discussions about whatever fascinates them. It could be music, sport or science, but there is sure to be a podcast for you. The format is growing all the time. In 2020, an estimated 100 million people listened to a podcast each month, and it's expected to reach 125 million in 2022. And they're not six seconds long either. The average podcast is around 45 minutes, with 75% of listeners tuning in to learn something new.

It truly is a new world.

This all means that the 'Six-Second Sensation' walks hand in hand with smart audience *segmentation*. Like many governments and businesses who had to navigate rapid organisation or societal change during the global pandemic, understanding your audience is the key to success. Intelligent and incisive opinion research is now a hallmark of communications Nimblicity.

As a result of this societal change in how we consume and exchange information, leaders don't always have the luxury of time to plan and develop how they want to communicate. Even if they choose not to, they need to be prepared to react and comment with a certain level of immediacy.

The British Airways 'free flights' bonanza

Just a few months after Mrs Thatcher's demise as the UK's first female prime minister was being arranged by her Conservative colleagues, a US-led coalition took on Iraq's former dictator Saddam Hussein for the first Gulf War.

The result of this conflict was catastrophic for airlines all around the world, and despite its market dominance at the time, British Airways was no exception to this. With pictures on every newspaper of one of its own aircraft burnt out on the tarmac at Kuwait Airport, US travellers decided that 1991 would be a good year for a staycation. Lord King, the British Airways chairman, remarked at the time that "The engine of consumer demand did not just idle in neutral, it sputtered to a complete stop.".

The reality was that all airlines needed to kick-start travel again, and British Airways developed a ground breaking marketing campaign to 'give away' 50,000 free tickets on the 23rd April 1991 to entice anxious customers to start flying in an era of terror attacks and war in the Middle East.

Less than two months after US-led coalition troops entered Kuwait, Lord King said to the waiting global media that "any fears of travel will evaporate with a free ticket." The world's biggest offer was launched globally in 70 countries on one day in March.

The public relations bonanza was only the beginning. The sheer volume of free tickets and scale of the endeavour made it a 'conversation starter'. In the pre-social media era, we remember people within the business (and outside) proudly talking about the give away in the staff canteens through to chats with friends in the local pub.

And with 30,000 BA employees enlisted as 'brand advocates', the story about getting people to start flying again took on a life of its own. It is estimated that some 500 million people read about the offer, 200 million saw it on TV and 5.7 million people entered the ballot for a free flight. And, most importantly for BA, passenger numbers returned to their original level within 120 days.

Imagine how that campaign would have played out in today's digitally connected world.

The success of BA back in 1991 was testimony to the strength of their planning and delivery being as nimble as possible in the environment at the time. Their ability to react quickly to the situation they found themselves in was the foundation for delivering a successful outcome. This was to get passengers flying again (remember, a good outcome is based on the audience doing something).

Going back to our ORACLE test – they had clear *outcomes*, a deep understanding of their *audience* (thanks to the launch of their Executive Club frequent flyer scheme in 1982), and they had crafted a compelling *story*.

While they didn't have the power of social media to engage people, they did recognise that the most effective channel would be through the age-old approach of 'word of mouth'. And loyal employees – both BA's strongest advocates as well as its fiercest critics – would soon spread the word of Lord King.

Objective – Story – Channels (OSC)

The most common problems we encounter from clients tend to flow from mixing up the tactical with the strategic, muddling a good strategy with a clear, over arching outcome. This happens for the same forgivable reasons so many of us 'lose track'. We are so buried with the daily routine and must do's that we forget what's really important. What, in the end, are we trying to accomplish here?

To answer this question, there is no greater weapon than what the Greeks call *ataraxia* or stillness/serenity. This is not some kind of 'New Age' quackery but rather forms part of the bedrock of successful strategic planning. All great leaders, from Abraham Lincoln to Sir Alex Ferguson, have recognised the vital importance of one's ability to ring fence time for *stillness* and thought. It sharpens perspective and illuminates connections. Of course, this can be a challenge in a 24/7 world where leaders are expected to communicate 365 days of the year.

If there is a single secret that we have learned from being in the room with some of the world's best known political and business leaders, it is this: that when the big decisions are made, it is they who seem to have a 'super power' to focus intently on the matter in hand. They are not necessarily more intelligent or numerate than subordinates; it is the clarity with which they can see the end goal.

Great leaders are able to give something their undivided attention, a quality that Sir Isaac Newton called 'the intended mind' – and not to go beyond that. If any of these folks had allowed themselves to dawdle in the grandiosity of their achievements or ambitions, they would never have left their bedrooms. The task in front of you is all that matters, whether it is communication or something else.

In the military, they call this simply 'The Process', and there has been a spate of textbooks recently on how successful army commanders and Seals communicate for victory. We would argue that there is no greater urgency or accuracy attached to communication than in the military. It is perhaps no surprise that it is here that we see some sensational examples of Nimblicity in (real) action. So, what are some of the tips and tricks from the military for nimble yet simple communication planning?

Firstly, army planners go through a process of evaluation, especially when confronted with Volatility, Uncertainty, Confusion and Ambiguity. The use of thoughtfulness and silence is often the most effective way to set out what you want to achieve.

As with our ORACLE test, what must come first is the *outcome* you are seeking to achieve; whether to take a province or drive up employee engagement throughout the workforce. Then, ensure you do your own research (even if informally through your own team), followed by an unambiguous strategy that has zero room for misinterpretation. And finally, draw up your plan of action that includes your channels, accepting that it will invariably not go according to plan, and be ready to adapt, modify and improvise.

Clear objectives

It is our job to develop strategies to win elections everywhere from Alabama to Australia, raise awareness of an 'issue', boost employee engagement, overthrow a dictator (although we failed at that one) and help change several global companies from the inside out. For each, our *first mission was to clearly define the outcome and then consider what objectives we need to have in order to succeed.*

In other words, answer the most fundamental questions first: what is it that you want to achieve? To raise awareness of a specific issue? Or to win a key seat at an election? Or one on the board?

This is more complicated than it may appear at first. For instance, to get a policy changed, you may believe you need to change the government. But, it may well be possible to achieve your outcome by having an objective to simply apply pressure on a few key politicians. The same principle applies in the commercial world. Look at the number of organisations that have changed the board or executive leadership team as a result of pressure from a small number of highly influential stakeholders. Rio Tinto was a prime example of this quite recently after the company inadvertently destroyed two 46,000-year-old ancient Aboriginal rock shelters in Western Australia.

One client asked us to help them engage their workforce with a new global strategy, but research found that the key blocker wasn't the substance of the strategy but the McKinsey-style language the company was using.

Or to cite a well-known example, you could argue that the second Iraq War was more a failure of clear *outcome-setting* than anything to do with faulty intelligence or oil interests. Was the goal to liberate Iraq? To disarm the dictator Saddam Hussein (as was the repeated rhetoric of the time) or remove him altogether (as many more argued *after* the event)? To build a democracy in the Arab world?

Or simply to remove the '45-minute threat' of the notorious weapons of mass destruction? All were advanced as our 'mission' at various times... and trust was eroded by such uncertainty almost from the get-go. There is nothing more important than a clear (and communicable) objective.

Your desired outcome will determine the strategy you need and the story you will therefore need to tell. Looking at it in political terms, we will begin any campaign by asking a simple set of questions to help us formulate the strategy:

- Who is going to decide the outcome? (i.e., which voters?)

- Where are they? (Both literally and figuratively – geographically and psychologically)

- What are the issues that matter to them?

- What do they need to hear from us if they are to be persuaded to join us/vote for us?

Our model for businesses communications – of a workforce – is very similar. Once you have established your outcome (to boost 'employee engagement', say), we would have a similar set of questions:

- Who is most critical to improving engagement?

- What are the critical 'issues' driving engagement?

- How do they understand and interpret those issues?

- What do they need to hear to think, feel and act differently?

Only when you have arrived at solid, stress-tested answers to these questions can you reasonably turn to the creation of a good strategic story.

Structuring your story

'Strategy' is one of the over used and least understood words in the English language today. Ask a dozen people how they define strategy, and you'll get a dozen different answers back. The lessons of good strategy depend on the discipline you're in. In communications, *there is nothing more important than your story*. Every story will be different necessarily. Nonetheless, each good, strategic story will pay acute attention to the emotions of an audience. And to be convincing and effective, it will possess several core components:

1. It needs to be grounded in reality

It will begin in a real world, recognisable to your audience, i.e. there is no point telling your workforce that your company is 'a great place to work' if they don't believe that. Similarly, political leaders arguing for change rarely pretend that everything their predecessors did before was awful (which makes perfect sense because why did so many people vote for them in the first place?). Donald Trump is an honourable exception to this rule.

2. It will have a logical flow, structure and an end point.

A story will have beginning, middle and end points. This means providing the context at the beginning, explaining what the journey will look and *feel* like and then painting a picture of what the destination will be if you come with us on this journey. In strategy terms, this will be your vision.

3. It will have a 'bad' guy

All engaging stories have protagonists (typically you, your leader or organisation) and antagonists (your competitor or adversary). Explaining who we are and *why we are different* to our opponents is an important aspect of creating an emotional *connection*. People typically bond with people who are similar to themselves.

Nicola Sturgeon, the leader of the Scottish National Party, played this incredibly well with her Tartan Army of voters. The antagonists in the story for Scottish independence are the Westminster Conservatives, who are deemed to be out of touch and insensitive to the needs of Scottish people.

4. It will set out *what* success looks like

Ultimately, people will want to know what positive benefits success will bring to them personally and the communities around them. They are less likely to be engaged by a promise of more profits and enhancing shareholder value (a common mistake made by way too many corporate clients) than they are hearing about themselves. *Personalise* the benefits.

5. It will be memorable

Going back to the 'Six-Second Sensation', a clear expression of strategy needs to be memorable and pithy. And this is where it gets tricky; after all, how sure can you be that all the key topics are covered in just three or four (and no more than five or six) points? This is deceptively difficult.

A strategy will likely mention the current mood, only one or two key issues, and *never* in shopping list form (which is a sure sign that you're getting far too tactical). Bill Clinton's 1992 presidential campaign is a fine example of strategic thinking in its purest form. To keep the campaign strategically aligned, his campaign manager James Carville hung a haiku-style sign in Clinton's Little Rock campaign headquarters which read simply:

1. Change versus more of the same

2. The economy, stupid

3. And don't forget healthcare

Such simplicity allows for flexibility and manoeuvrability in the face of changing events, crises or challenges. It allows for the simple truth that planning and delivery of your communication must be *nimble*.

Channels – How to best reach your audience?

If having a clear objective is akin to setting the destination for your journey, and a strategy sets how you will get there, then your communications *channels* are where the rubber truly hits the road. These are the avenues you will use to engage: email, leaflets, video conferencing, face-to-face, etc. The right use of channels is as vital as a smart strategy and the right objective.

Your audience will determine the right mix of channels for you. Where are they? How do they get most of their information at present? What sources do they *trust*? This is the point where many communications managers will reach for their 'Social Media Toolbox'... but this should *not* be automatic. Instead, the governing rule of thumb should be 'What is most convenient for *them*, not for us?'

For instance, we have worked for many businesses with a company Intranet that is hopelessly ineffective. In those circumstances, it may be advisable to use a different medium (or create an entirely new one). Similarly, during a recent Australian campaign in a predominantly non-English-speaking electorate, understanding what these voters were listening to (and in what language) was critical to our success. You have to make it as easy as possible for *them* to engage with you.

LAW OF NIMBLICITY #6:

MATCH YOUR MESSAGE TO THE MOMENT

"The single biggest problem with communication is the illusion that it has taken place at all."

George Bernard Shaw

We have examined how there is nothing more important than the story you are telling an audience. Every story will be different. And each good, strategic story will contain a clear, concise and compelling *message* to those you seek to influence. What is your 'pitch', in essence? What do you wish to change? *And what do you want THEM to do?*

These are the key questions of your message and in any campaign — whether it is political or business, message matters most of all.

The importance of recall

Why do a select few words, phrases and sayings stick relentlessly in our minds, while others – identical in length, tonality or brevity – dissolve like steam evaporating on a summer's day? The latter are, obviously, far more common… which is what makes the former so invaluable to professional communicators and campaigners. We seek out those words, phrases and feelings that stick – those that we recall without our trying or wishing to.

> *'Beans Meanz Heinz'.*
> *'Yes, we can'.*
> *'A Mars a Day…'*
> *'Because you're worth it'.*

The practice is well-established in FMCG (Fast-Moving Consumer Goods) research, but think of electoral affairs also. For instance, throughout 2016's seismic US election, researchers would ask if people had heard, read or seen anything about Hillary Clinton. Then separately, whether they'd heard anything about Donald Trump – not their policies or positions, especially… but their perceptions. If the person being interviewed said they had, interviewers asked them what they recalled about the candidate.

Gallup found that the most frequent words that people recalled about Hillary Clinton were 'email', 'FBI', 'investigation', 'foundation', and 'scandal'. For Trump, the words most closely connected were the words he wanted voters to remember: 'Economy, business, jobs', 'make America great again'… and (just occasionally…) 'Lock her up'.

In the commercial world, branding experts have known for many years the power and influence of having a catchy, memorable slogan. They are easy to deride, but the 'Just Do It' campaign helped to take our old friends at Nike from 18% to 43% market share in ten years. 'A Diamond is Forever' catapulted De Beers sales by 55% in three years. 'The Ultimate Driving Machine' took BMW from the 11th largest European import marque in the United States to the #1 luxury car brand. Coke – simply sugar-saturated water – has elevated this over a century to a virtual art form ('Taste the Feeling' began in 1906 as 'The Great National Temperance Beverage', believe it or not).

These supposedly simple statements work so well because they invoke whole *stories* in our minds. The words are not really what it is about. In the adage of advertising, 'We aren't selling products, but FEELINGS'. Memorable messages are crafted for the ear. Just like the nursery rhymes we first heard as kids, the strongest messages are almost melodic. Once you've heard it a couple of times you can easily recall and repeat it.

Bypassing our prefrontal cortex (the 'thinking' bit of the brain), our emotions are stirred up, just out of our line of sight – one reason why these 'hooks' are better thought of as entire strategies rather than taglines or slogans. And just picture how differently you might look at Nike if they had gone to market under the banner of 'Just Go For It'… if BMW had alighted on 'The Ultimate Car'… or the effect wrought if De Beers had decided that 'Diamonds Are for a Long Time'.

How often do the leaders of companies truly understand the importance and impact of their message? Surprisingly seldom, in our experience. Take a recent project we led for a major energy company based in the UK and North America: out of 45 conversations with senior executives, *only one* of them could accurately reflect the core strategic messages of the company they were supposed to be leading. And that was the group CEO. "I don't understand because we communicated it extensively," was his response. And it is understandable why he felt that way, as they did indeed have an extensive (and expensive) internal communications campaign.

We find this to be a massive recurring problem in big organisations. The conversation typically goes along the following lines:

Us: Do you have a strategy?

CEO: Yes, of course.

Us: Have you communicated it?

CEO: Yes, we shared this (and out comes the classic management consultants' deck, comprising around 1,000 incomprehensible slides).

Us: What is more important to you: creating awareness that you have a strategy or having a strategy message that is remembered and understood?

CEO: … [Blank expression, then looks expectantly at rapidly whitening in-house communication professional].

Or take an example from academia. When researchers from the University of Technology in Sydney asked employees of 20 major Australian corporations – with clearly articulated public strategies – to identify their employer's strategy from among six choices, just 29% answered correctly. And the trouble is – if you think you've said your piece, but your audience hasn't 'got it'… it is not their problem – it's *yours*.

The scientific answer to this lies in what psychologists refer to as our sensory memory, which relates to the five major senses of touch, taste, sight, hearing and smell. Think about it for a moment. The feeling of sand in your toes can evoke a memory of a favourite holiday. The smell of a cologne that an ex-partner wore. The taste of a food that made you ill. Going back to a place you haven't been to for years. These buried sensations and feelings are the treasure of the effective communicator.

The recall rule – conciseness, clarity and 'chunks'

THE RECALL RULE:

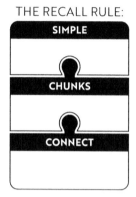

The importance of communication brevity has been around for many years... surprisingly when you consider how often we get stuck listening to someone with a microphone, wondering, 'Will this ever end?' Consider how often the opposite occurs.

Thomas Jefferson once said, "The most valuable of all talents is that of never using two words when one will do." More recently, David Rock from the NeuroLeadership Institute contended that if something takes less than three seconds to say to yourself or say out loud... it is *significantly* easier to recall and use. Any time you craft an idea that you want people to remember easily, if the idea can be said out loud in under three seconds, the chances of usage go up dramatically.

While brevity is key, the ability to recall words in order also depends on several characteristics of these words. We have sometimes deployed the mnemonic 'SIMPLE CHUNKS CONNECT' when thinking about this.

SIMPLE everyday words are more familiar and therefore more effective than jargon or abstract language. Don't use a convoluted or 'clever-sounding' word when a short one will do.

CHUNK your messages into small pieces of information to make reading and understanding faster and easier. This is the whole purpose of what became known as 'paragraphs', incidentally.

CONNECT words that sound similar to each other (this is called the phonological similarity effect) or words that can create a meaningful connection.

In the 1930s, Hollywood movie studios concluded that people need to hear about their movies at least seven times before wanting to see the latest release. This led to the 'Rule of Seven' theory in marketing, whereby a consumer needs to hear about something at least seven times before they'll take action to buy that product or service. Some of these are subliminal – for instance, that poster you see on your commute home from work may not be the point at which you 'chose to purchase'… but it served an invaluable purpose, keeping that product, brand or service close to the front of your mind.

However, mindless repetition alone does not build memory – it is vital to note that quality, type and timing of repetition are each as important as quantity. So, how do you ensure they remember what you say? The answer lies in what is known as 'spaced repetition'.

The German psychologist Hermann Ebbinghaus discovered back in the late 1890s that human beings typically forget around 40% of any information within 20 minutes of first hearing it. They will then only remember about 25% of the original information after one day and then down to about 10% after a month. Thus, our brain is more likely to label information as important if it has been repeated (not straight away) but at spaced intervals. Each time this is done brings the message recall back to 100% and, over a period of time it becomes firmly embedded into our memory.

Message in a bottle

When we work with clients to plan a campaign – for a candidate, company or charity – we live by a simple, tactical maxim: Message Matters Most. Whether you are 're-tooling the business to be fit for the 21st century'… 'the candidate of change' or simply, 'Save the Koalas', your message is the most important thing about you. Whether your priority is 'Making the world a cleaner place' – say – or 'Ending Islamophobia', it is vital that you:

a) Establish what your message is.

b) Translate into language that is properly understood by the people who will determine your success.

In practice, that is the purpose of something we call a message matrix.

The message matrix is a straightforward device – a set of questions – to help you to understand what they are likely to say: how they will represent themselves – and you – to the people you need to win over and, therefore, which facts and emotions you will need to marshal in order to respond as effectively as possible.

Here's how it works in practice:

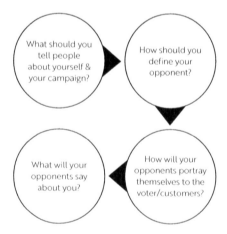

Remember too that language is a different concept than the message.

Talking about 'reducing unemployment rates' and 'getting you your job back' are conveying essentially the same message. However, *linguistically* they are at opposite poles. We must *personalise, humanise* and *empathise* wherever possible – as we explore in more depth in the following chapter. This can be a real problem, as you will know if you have run a day-long board seminar on human resources compliance or been part of a cabinet discussion on foreign policy with China.

Be conscious of the next step of the process – translating that into terms that are *relevant to your audience*. Use language to ensure you are talking about people. The effect of simply 'reframing' in this way can be dynamite.

Secondly, consider more deeply than any other aspect, 'How does a message fit in with the broader *story* you are telling?' What are you trying, ultimately, to do? We live in a world of more personal autonomy than we have ever had, and thus, the search for our meaning has deepened too. Whereas in earlier eras, the objectives we sought from our job – or our governments – were prosaic (to keep us safe and well-fed, maybe a little wealthier than our parents were before us), today it is striking how often these expectations are confounded. We seem to want more than a job, a tax cut and to be left alone.

If you can speak to something deeper than those of the most basic safety and security – while ensuring that these are met, of course – you will attain a far deeper bond of loyalty and trust from those you seek to lead. Research today allows you to tap into this richer soil, to understand better the ambitions of your audience. As one prominent psychologist puts it memorably, "all people serve their ambition. In that matter, there are no atheists. There are only people who know, and don't know, what God they serve." Being honest and, yes, authentic about your own meaning can narrow the often seemingly unbridgeable divide between leaders and followers.

First, we must have the fundamental humility to accept that we *don't* have all the answers ourselves – which is why one of the most emotionally engaging parts of any campaign communication is the call to *action* – asking for their help. By inviting others to share in the story you are trying to create, you are tapping into a force far greater than any individual understands. This is the potency of stories; 'we are the ones we've been looking for' has never been truer or more necessary.

Second, have the courage to share more of yourself and your story, and you will find that more of the answers already lie in front of you. Through *turning 'I' stories into 'we' stories*, lasting change is achieved, communities are transformed and governments are overthrown.

Message or mess-enger...?

While controversy has forced many a boss from their mahogany desk – Martin Winterkorn at VW and Travis Kalanick at Uber, for instance – it is interesting how seldom strong 'favourability' or ratings correlate with CEOs keeping their jobs. Or, for that matter, prime ministers and presidents being good at their jobs. Some of our most dynamic and successful politicians spent most (Margaret Thatcher, for instance) or *all* (e.g. Australia's Paul Keating) of their time at the top with a net favourability score that was 'underwater' (i.e. less than zero). Nonetheless, both won thumping majorities because – in the end – the message is more important than the messenger.

Donald Trump is another notorious example. Apart from the very first week of his administration, significantly more Americans *disapproved* of the way the 45th president was doing his job than approved. Intriguingly, this number included many who ended up voting for him anyway. The deeper lesson is that audiences – whether voters or employees – tend to prefer those who *stake out their position clearly*, in primary colours, over those who prevaricate and posture. This remains the case, even if it is one that they disagree with.

Ronald Reagan only came close to matching the public's 'approval' of his successor, Jimmy Carter, in the aftermath of his being gunned down at the Washington Hilton. Reagan's good-humoured response to the actions of a demented gunman – prompting his ER surgeons with a twinkle, "I hope you're all Republicans…" – endeared him to Americans and showed that he was far from the feeble fossil his opponents had attempted to portray. Despite a gruelling recession of the early 1980s and persistent high unemployment, he was rewarded with a re-election landslide victory in 1984, allowing him to promise America, "you ain't seen nothin' yet."

Following on in a similar vein, some of the most effective *business* language that we coach is decidedly 'anti-business'. Great political language is often 'anti-political' to most normal people's ears… at which Reagan was a past master. In part, this is simply that ability to communicate complex ideas in simple language. Using a unique mix of metaphor and imagery, humour and homespun philosophy, Reagan especially understood 'never to "talk down" to his audience… it was always on the level of a peer or colleague'. Business leaders should take note. In that sense, he was an (unwitting) forefather of this Law of Nimblicity.

Deploying aspiration

In 1990, as the last embers of his comic genius faded away, the legendary Dudley Moore starred in a rapidly forgotten 'comedy caper', *Crazy People*. The central premise of the movie is of an advertising executive who loses his mind… and ultimately starts dreaming up slogans that 'level with people'… or simply tell the truth.

Some of the slogans Dud's character proposes – "Jaguar: The car for men who want hand jobs from beautiful women they hardly know," "The French can be annoying – come to Greece instead!" and, "Volvo: they're boxy, but they're good!" – are hilarious because they deliberately miss out the one ingredient that is essential to winning communication: *aspiration*.

We don't want to hear about the problems we already know about, even if they might be critical. Volvos *are* boxy – the gag wouldn't be funny if they weren't – but we find it funny that the business could ever acknowledge this simple truth. Some companies have adopted this approach; it has rarely been successful.

Even in troubled times, we are drawn to those who appeal 'to the better angels of our nature', in Abraham Lincoln's own demonstration of the technique. We remain suckers for 'the triumph of hope over experience' or simply to the promise of a better future. As with salespeople, we are instinctively drawn to those who help us to feel good about ourselves, our community or our country. We struggle to buy from, or vote for, people we *don't* like.

Just think of any number of recent famous 'calls to action':

> *'Yes, we can'.*
> *'Make America Great Again'.*
> *'Believe in better'.*
> *'Come stand with me'.*
> *'Take the Pepsi Challenge'.*
> *'Australia deserves better'.*
> *'Because you're worth it…'*

Hope alone does not make a winning message, but without aspiration in the mix, your recipe will be missing a vital ingredient. It is one of the foundations that separates public communication – whether voter-facing campaigns or programmes of change within large organisations – from our private deliberations and discussions.

We all know the banal truths about our lives, the struggles that we face and may never overcome. We look to our leaders to lift our gaze – in our work and our world – whether we know it or not. In the same way that we expect the person on the stage to look a little, well… better than us, we need them to be more aspirational too. Why else would we follow them?

There is, of course, a great trade-off at play here. Paint too rosy a picture, and you will forfeit *credibility* and trust. Rather like dealing with a car salesperson, we don't wish to be taken for fools. We understand that the transformation from poverty to wealth… depression to ecstasy… second-rater to global winner… is not likely to be simple or straightforward. But here's the thing: we still need to hear a bit of it if we are to *buy* what you are saying.

Fellow football fans of underachieving teams will understand the sentiment of, 'it's not the despair that gets me… it's the hope!' Real change is hard. Anyone attempting to lose weight, stop drinking, become more productive at work, tolerant at home or attain that elusive 'six-pack' knows this deeply. And yet, we still fall prey to the 'quick-fix' merchants and mendacious sales routines.

As in our private lives, so we are professionally. They may be honest, but the CEO who talks frankly about employees facing a 'bitter pill to swallow' will likely be damned compared to the one who trumpets easy solutions. And many is the political leader to have risen on a tide of 'hope and change', only to find the realities of introducing real reform – Obamacare, say, or delivering Global Britain – are much tougher than advertised.

The need to balance aspiration and reality is never-ending. Part of the trick is to keep an element of 'play' involved. Don't get too closely immersed in the details of the problem you are trying to solve. Instead, keep yourself focused on 'the big picture' and the brighter future. "To bring power, the fantasy must remain on some level distant and problem-free," Robert Greene wrote in *The 48 Laws of Power*. Too much granularity grinds an audience down. Forget the importance of *aspiration* at your peril.

Stockholm syndrome

Levels of aspiration – and emotionalism more broadly – will depend, in part, on geography. Sweden, as one example from our recent experience, is a country that stockpiles contradictions. Ask an American how they feel about a particular issue on a scale of one to ten, and it is no exaggeration to say that many will plump for '11'. Many Europeans these days are not far behind, whether France's *gilets jaunes* or Britain's ever-feuding tribes of Brexiteers and Remainers. Swedes, on the other hand, will routinely respond to almost any message with a 'four', 'five' or 'six', at most. This is a country where the answer to almost any question is, "*Well, it depends.*"

It is one of the Nordic countries routinely cited by liberals and left-wingers as the kind of 'equal, fairer' place that the rest of us should seek to emulate. But it is also one of the most dynamic, entrepreneurial countries on Earth. Roughly the same size as Greece, Sweden has given us IKEA, electronics giant Ericsson, Volvo, clothing giant H&M, manufacturers Skanska (recent rebuilders of LaGuardia Airport), Saab, Scania and Spotify. The Swedes don't 'punch above their weight' entrepreneurially speaking so much as stop everyone else in the first round.

The Swedish state itself is known as 'the Bumblebee' because, in the same way as the big-bodied/small-winged Apidae shouldn't be able to fly… it does so, quite happily. Similarly, Swedes accept relatively high taxation (close to 60% top rate) in return for top-rate public services. According to standard free-market economics, Sweden should struggle to stay airborne too. Yet, it does not. But even here, we found the tectonic plates shifting beneath our petty preconceptions and the message from Swedish people themselves sharpening in tone.

After 2011/12's Arab Spring, the influx of over one million refugees was portrayed in the media as creating a hostile political environment in the country. We found anything but. Instead, they called their country a "miracle," "outward-looking" and a "blossoming... model for others to follow."

Although they acknowledged that there were problems with education, housing costs and migrants, the prevailing sentiment was "we have to help these people to integrate." They emphatically did *not* wish to 'send them packing'. Instead, what was striking was the sheer level of *optimism* that Swedish people felt about their country. Like Botswanans and South Africans, they felt that things were getting better – especially if the politicians would act on the biggest challenges they face... "and leave us to get on with the rest of it."

Such aspirational, 'anti-political' language has always been seductive and is even more so in the modern world of democratised distrust. Politics and politicians seem to conduct themselves in a language all of their own. Few, if any of us, truly understand it. What does 'tax reform' actually mean? Who are 'stakeholders' exactly? When someone emerges who appears to *speak our language*, that engages our hopes without even having to think about it.

The Story Staircase™

In the end, all of a campaign's output – the language, the visuals, the channels and all the rest – should be designed to support a central 'story' about what you want to change. Drew Westen was writing about elections specifically, but the principles he identified are as relevant to us whether applied to an NGO, charity or driving organisational change within a big business.

Whether they know it or not, your audience's choice will be overwhelmingly based upon:

1. A campaign's 'master narrative'.

2. The person who is most likeable and emotionally resonant (i.e. charismatic).

3. The person with attributes likely to make them successful leaders.

And when you're deciding on a piece of communication – whether ad, email, newsletter or speech – the bottom line is emotional. So a pithy test to run it through is this: *If they can't feel it, don't use it.*

Now, of course, for many in business and politics, the word 'story' can sound a bit hokey... or even be seen as downright childish. There are simply too many occasions where the very mention of the word has caused hard-bitten executives' eyes to glaze over while thinking of ways to exit the meeting, by window if necessary. And this makes some sense; there are plenty of sharp-suited operators willing to charge a big buck to produce a 'story' that is no more effective – and often a good deal less so – than what you could've accomplished alone.

It is difficult to figure out, methodically and meticulously, what must go into a compelling, credible and consistent story – and what really shouldn't. As an aside, people at the top of big organisations – whether big companies or political parties – do not tend to be the kind of people who make 'natural' storytellers in any case. But that is no reason to put yourself at an unnecessary disadvantage.

All campaigns and change management efforts involve the careful marshalling of resources: people, money and time. While businesspeople depend on nothing more than a tried, trusted and tested process for problem-solving. It is for these reasons that we developed the Story Staircase™ methodology in order to help leaders construct their own stories as efficiently and effectively as possible.

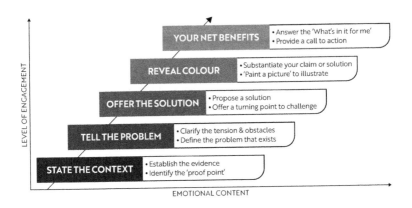

There are five distinct steps to the Staircase all based around the acronym STORY:

S: State the context – Context tells us where we are, which is why the first step of the Staircase revolves around the 'why we have to change…' This will require a mixture of both what Aristotle called *pathos* (an appeal to the emotions) and *logos* (appeals to reason). In plain English, this means that you need to set out the facts. But not just any old facts. We require the facts that matter to your audience – the provable points that ultimately stir the emotions.

It seems that 99 times out of 100 when we ask clients for 'the facts' (i.e. the key facts that support their argument), they respond with assumptions. We assemble 'facts' to reinforce our pre-existing emotional biases. For example, they will tell us things like "our marketplace is more competitive" without backing that statement up. This isn't factual – it's a perceived insight – and so the challenge is to get them to talk about the facts that led them to this assumption. Once they start talking facts, they begin to organise the evidence that backs up their actions.

It is no surprise that most employees say that change is managed badly in their organisation – in nearly five decades of combined experience of big organisations, we have never encountered a group that has told us that change has been well-managed. So often, this is because leadership hasn't been able to 'explain the why'.

II: **Talk about the problem (or challenge)** – It's extraordinary how difficult it can be to answer the simplest of questions: what is the problem or challenge we need to fix, and why am I the right person to meet that challenge? The next challenge is to write it in a concise form, normally in two to three sentences where it can pass the Twitter 280-character test.

III: **Offer the solution** – In other words, what are the changes or policies you intend to implement? Because of the ways in which our brains are structured, the practical/policy piece should be a significantly smaller portion of your communication than the first step (and the shortest step on the Staircase overall).

Your challenge now is two fold. First, you need to explain exactly what you intend to do (the actions). Second, it must link directly to what's in it for me and/or others. Get this right, and you see the magic of bringing others with you. But they will be reluctant to engage unless they KNOW what benefits it will bring – in tangible, believable terms.

IV: **Reveal some colour** – After you have shared the solution, pivot to the future. What does 'success' look – and feel – like? What will be in it for you and all of us if you come on this journey with us? The more you can personalise, the better. Metaphor and analogy work especially well here. Over the years, we have induced executives to literally paint pictures, use photographs, bring in personal artefacts, make movies, sing songs… all in the name of untapping their creative side to explain what they actually mean when they say certain things.

V: **Your call to action** – All great communication should deliver an outcome – whether it's putting the X in the ballot box for the aspiring political leader, seeking an investor to make a financial commitment or a business leader who wants their employees to change the way they work.

Making a message live and breathe

What does putting all this together in practice look like? Well, we had the privilege of working with (Lord) Sebastian Coe and the London Organising Committee of the Olympic and Paralympic Games (LOCOG) for what could have been an incredibly tedious 'brand values'/corporate PR-type event.

Instead, Coe arrived at Lord's Cricket Ground and told his own personal story about having watched the Olympics in Mexico as a child and dreamed of being an athlete and winning a gold medal. This was similar to the pitch he made to the IOC when London won the Games in 2005, but this time he aligned it to the LOCOG's vision and values.

Putting Lord Coe's communications as a leader through the ORACLE test, his outcome was clear. He wanted the 400 people working at LOCOG to believe in his dream and feel as inspired as he was. The goal was for this story – Coe's own – to provide the aspirational lift that would act as the catalyst for making his Olympic dream come alive to every person who joined the LOCOG organisation thereafter – ceding control to all 70,000 volunteer 'Games Makers' that the games depended upon – and leverage their personal stories of involvement to ensure that the 2012 Olympic Games would become a true British success story.

And as Coe said after the Olympic flame was extinguished,

> *"The volunteers really are the unsung heroes of communities across the UK and were fundamental to the success of the Games this summer. The determination of the Games Makers to do something special for their city and country and for the athletes of the UK and the world helped to make the Games an unforgettable experience for everyone who was at the Games in 2012. They continue to inspire us all."*

Each step on the Story Staircase was essential to the combined impact of 'the whole'. And each led inexorably to the next, clearest reiteration of your objective. Your message. It doesn't matter how sleek your 'meme machine' is or your flash ads… unless they enhance and clarify the core of what you must get across.

While the message that Coe delivered was incredibly compelling and drew his audience in to listen more, the *authenticity* of his delivery touched an emotional nerve and made it even more inspirational.

In our experience, the cocktail of a powerful story delivered with authenticity is a combination that can win over the most cynical of people. Added to that is an intuitive sense of timing – Coe's words fit *the moment* absolutely perfectly. And it is this unique combination that helps demonstrate why message matters more today than ever.

LAW OF NIMBLICITY #7:

HUMANISE, PERSONALISE AND EMPATHISE IN ORDER TO CONNECT

"Your time is limited, so don't waste it living someone else's life... Don't let the noise of opinions drown out your own voice... Have the courage to follow your heart and intuition. They somehow already know what you TRULY want to become. Everything else is secondary."

Steve Jobs

While the means have changed, the principle of understanding your *audience* is about as novel a concept as the wheel. Aristotle, a name we cite repeatedly for the sheer brilliant simplicity of his art of rhetoric, literally made it the 'A' of his 'A, B, C' of intelligent communication. He advises his readers to "avail themselves of some knowledge of their intended interlocutors." In other words, if you're hoping to influence an audience – be it a group of difficult engineers, swing voters or a committee of directors interviewing you for a job – then it certainly helps if you know they're going to like what you say.

However, another ancient law of politics and government also reverberates down the ages and bears repeating at this point. Those who attempt to chase popularity for its own sake – in the boardroom or at the ballot box – will likely be punished for it. We don't respond well to people pleasers. If an audience is listening to you, they expect you to be *leading* them somewhere, even if they don't like everything about where it is you're intending to go.

This is only a 'macro' manifestation of something that happens every day on the micro level. Think of the people you trust and would turn to for a crucial piece of advice or counsel. It is a fairly safe bet that this person would not necessarily be the person you would expect to tell you what you'd like to hear. Of course, neither would it be someone you thought a complete phoney or people pleaser.

When you dwell upon it, it's a unique mixture of qualities and aspects that person would embody, is it not? And it is these qualities that are the hallmark of Nimblicity.

Let's take a couple of well-known examples. A recent YouGov survey in the UK showed that the broadcaster and environmentalist Sir David Attenborough is 'the most liked person in Britain' after seven decades of nature programmes, with a 'favourability rating' of 87%.

The second Briton on the list is the children's author Roald Dahl, only narrowly behind Sir David with 81%. Dahl was indeed one of Britain's favourite authors, including our own. He was also an anti-Semite and, by all accounts, a pretty awful husband, christened

'Roald the Rotten' by his first wife for his various extramarital affairs.

But the point here is not to disparage the name of the beloved author of *James and the Giant Peach*, rather to note how little we know of those in public life who we profess to love. Despite our lack of real knowledge about what people are truly like behind closed doors, you will almost certainly have strong feelings about what you think people in public life are *like*.

The perception test

When it comes to influencing people, what is more important? Is it the content of your words or what they feel you are 'like'? Your rational mind may well respond in the former, but from psychologists, neuroscientists, as well as our own, innumerable studies of voters and employee sentiment in every corner of the globe, it's clear that we base our opinion on the latter.

We can speak for hours on what we think about someone, the CEO, the Prime Minister or a prominent public figure. But ask us to recall something significant that they have said, and we would struggle to muster more than a sentence or two – which is odd when you consider how well we feel we 'know' them.

To prove the point, you can try something that we have done with *hundreds* of leaders that we have coached over the years:

First of all, think of a well-known political or business figure from recent history: maybe somebody like Tony Blair, Elon Musk, Hillary Clinton or Bill Gates.

Once you have that person pictured in your mind, write down any phrases or words that you can remember them saying. Most people tend to find this quite difficult.

Next, consider any words or phrases that describe what you think that person is *like*.

If you are like most of the population – and indeed, like most leaders that we coach – you will quickly have a reasonable list of words with only a bare modicum of effort.

When we ask people about Tony Blair, for instance, you would be amazed at the level of passion aroused in our fellow Brits. Some people will recall Blair talking about the weapons of mass destruction, but a surprising number also remember the introduction of the minimum wage, Sure Start and peace in Northern Ireland.

More importantly, they tend to gravitate away from what he said towards what they believe he is like. So Blair's detractors will use words like 'slimy', 'faker' and 'liar'. Those with more moderate or positive views describe him as 'talented', 'unifier' and 'a people person'.

The point of the exercise is what people say – they *believe* to be true. They are statements of perceptions, not facts. And equally, it illustrates that most people will quickly forget what people say – do you remember our mnemonic 'Simple Chunks Connect' and the Ebbinghaus theory in the last chapter? We will not be offended if you have forgotten it already… it simply reinforces the point.

What we do know from the research we have conducted over the years with employees, customers and voters is that most people will vividly remember what they perceive to be true.

Machiavelli perhaps understood this better than anybody. After all, his own *name* was turned into an insult by his detractors.

What do *you* think when you hear the word 'Machiavellian'? Cunning, perhaps. Deceitful… Manipulative. Perhaps his famous quote that, "the ends justify the means." Only, Machiavelli *never* wrote or said those words. Nor did he preach deception or wickedness. Far from it. What he did was to set out the norms and laws of politics as he observed them, rather than had been set out by church dogma. Much the same as Galileo did with physics and astronomy, in fact. And for speaking those truths, Machiavelli was to suffer a similar fate at the hands of Rome, finding his name blackened and his books banned for centuries.

"Men judge generally more by the eye than by the hand, for everyone can see, and few can feel. Everyone sees what you appear to be; few really know what you are," he wrote – and nobody has put it better since.

Watching your CEO speak or a presidential debate, you may be struck by a familiar feeling. How do I know if this person is 'for real'? Was that moment 'authentic' or something clever that they had pre-planned for effect? Take heart – people have been wondering the same thing for *millennia*.

Connecting this back to our ORACLE test, if you are a leader, reflect on the perception test for yourself by asking, *would my audience remember what I have said and what would they say about me as a person?*

This will be an important part of your research, for as Aristotle advocated in his art of rhetoric, if you as the speaker don't have 'ethos' (or personal credibility), then why on earth should your audience listen to you?

In this chapter, we want to explore some of the key aspects of staying personal, human and *authentic*, as well as the risks of fakery.

Having authentic dialogue

Arun Sarin was born in Pachmarhi in India, the son of an Indian military officer. After attending a military boarding school in

Bangalore (now India's answer to Silicon Valley), he went on to live and study in the United States. In 2003, Sarin was appointed Group CEO of Vodafone, which, at the time, was the world's largest mobile telecommunications company.

Despite being founded in 1991, Vodafone witnessed spectacular global growth through its 'Hunt or be Hunted' strategy in the late 1990s and early 2000s. The game changer was the hostile US$180.9 billion purchase in 2000 of Mannesmann AG, the 200-year-old German conglomerate. This was and is still the largest corporate acquisition in history.

But growth by acquisition is a path fraught with tales of lost synergies, 'silo mentalities' and costly divorces later on. Sarin was absolutely rigid that this must not happen and sent a signal early on that he would prioritise connecting with employees over and above anyone else.

As he explained on his first day to the corporate affairs director who was keen to line up financial PR interviews and an investor relations road trip, "If we don't get the communication with our people right and connect with them, then we won't have a business to talk about to our external friends."

Not only did Arun want to talk to employees directly, but he also wanted to actively listen to what they were talking about so that he could match his message and voice with the prevailing mood of the organisation. His guidance at the time was for his internal communication team to become his eyes and ears as opposed to being his internal spokespeople.

The internal dialogue within the Vodafone community had to come first. And he was committed to it, even if it meant hearing some things he didn't want to because, as he said, "Look, at times they're going to be our fiercest critics, but they're our biggest advocates too. If I've engaged them, then everything else follows on from that."

And this mantra went to the extreme of Sarin's own direct message to the business, a monthly email from Arun to all employees called 'Arun's Corner'. This was an early version of what would today be called a blog. It was a personal and insightful view from the top, which was stuffed full of so-called 'Arun-isms'. These were charmingly Indian-American words and phrases that (Vodafone was still overwhelmingly a British company, remember) only Arun would ever use.

The effect was electric.

This is something we've seen time and time again when the people realise that it's really him or her doing the writing. Whether it's a blog, newsletter or tweet, we have sat next to a prime minister, presidential candidate or CEO when they have communicated directly, and the visitor numbers jump when word gets around that they're chatting directly with their leader. It's unmistakable (which incidentally also helps to explain President Trump's remarkable social media 'pull').

All the typos and crazy all-caps rants may have political journalists clutching their pearls, but for the average voter, it tells you that it really is 'The Donald' at the other end of this thing.

Contrast this to a time at Nike in 1999 when Phil Knight started to host an early version of live webchats with employees. The opportunity to chat directly with Phil led to Nike's internal IT systems crashing as so many people tried to join at the specified day and time. Sadly, the initiative didn't last long when word got out that Phil wasn't actually at the end of the keyboard typing in the responses. It was all done by the slick efforts of the corporate communications team.

Interestingly, Vodafone's PR and legal teams insisted on cleaning up 'Arun's Corner' by taking out all the 'Arun-isms' and his personal reflections. They did this to mitigate the risk of his messages being misinterpreted by the media, but the result was that employee interest in it just *plummeted*. It shifted from being an authentic, personal voice to one that was overtly 'corporate' and was eventually pulled in favour of video messages where Arun could revert to being his genuine, authentic self again.

Channelling 'their' voice

Like Arun, who could not have been more different to the employees at Vodafone, you don't need to be 'of' the people to speak *to the people's* hopes and dreams for a better future. It took Bernie Sanders, a Jewish septuagenarian from Brooklyn, to tap into millennial frustration with Hillary Clinton and the traditional political elite.

Another New Yorker, the gilded billionaire Donald Trump effortlessly tapped into the same beliefs and emotions of his blue-collar audience, despite having virtually no first hand knowledge of the daily struggles they face.

Winston Churchill himself was an unashamed imperialist and aristocrat yet could speak to 'the common man' and, more vitally, express his underlying emotional *spirits* with uncommon ease. Arguably, Boris Johnson has a similar gift to his Conservative hero (albeit by nothing like the degree he would wish), to the eternal and enduring frustration of Labour party stalwarts.

Through digital and social media, we are encouraged to rush more quickly to judgment than ever before. We are interested in a greater range of people and topics, even as we are less impressed by what we hear. The upbraiding of various British celebrities, such as Stacey Dooley – labelled as having 'white saviour' complexes for her programmes for an astonishingly aspirational Comic Relief fundraiser – is just one recent example.

We look less today to 'celebrity endorsers' than we do to people who *look like us*. One reason for this is that if we want to imagine doing something in the future, then we need to see ourselves in the picture today. This means that the 'stars' of the modern internet age – the bloggers and vloggers; the kings and queens of YouTube – are strikingly ordinary folk, broadcasting from their bedrooms and broom closets.

Fascinatingly, if we have noticed one kind of backlash recently, it's from the 'authentic online community' pushing back against established stars 'piggy backing' their success on social media sites. There is something altogether less tangible and relatable about the success of pre-established stars cashing in online.

Behavioural psychologists have shown that fear of loss exerts about twice the pull on us as the hope for change. The same is true in business as well. Employees are far more likely to engage with 'saving our jobs' than 'restructuring for our future'. Hence the trade unions typically getting the upper hand on management when it comes to engaging employees with *change*.

Despite this, it is a particular feature of many internal communications campaigns to leave this 'tangible benefits' component out altogether. It is frightening how often we have consulted for organisations, or speechwriters or electoral runs that have forgotten to spell out exactly *what's in it for the audience* in an aspirational, emotional way.

In an increasingly digital, commoditised world where we can feel ever more automated and atomised, feeling and speaking 'human' is a valuable skill set for smart businesses.

Good 'EQ' is now a winning USP

Picture the scene somewhere in the American Midwest in the early noughties. The US economy was sputtering into a recession. The first wave of 'dot coms' crashed on the shores of a Nasdaq stock melt down, aided by global insecurity and the messy aftermath of the Gulf War. Millions of jobs were lost while worker pay crawled along, barely growing at all. "We're told low wages are the reality if we're going to compete abroad," as Bob Dylan sardonically sang at the time in *Modern Times*. There were few more potent, polarising symbols of unbridled US capitalism than the Bentonville, Arkansas-based, family-built retail empire of Walmart.

The 'Wake Up Walmart' campaign was founded by the United Food and Commercial Workers Union in 2005 with a focus to hammer the company on a range of issues from low wages, working practices and overseas sourcing of products.

It was so effective *precisely* because it tapped into community frustration by asking the questions that people felt strongly about. Do we really want our goods produced at the absolute lowest cost, regardless of what that may entail for the workers who produce or retail them? Should the ability of massive, multi-billion-dollar companies to effectively drive competitors out of business really be unrestricted?

Of course, such questions are values-laden, but that didn't matter when the anger of consumer groups, unions, churchgoers and environmentalists was *real*. Furthermore, Wake Up Walmart cleverly directed them at elected officials, who felt pressured to 'make a stand'. As one of the campaign's leaders put it, "We had genuine, community-driven passion on our side. We'd have events, press releases and political outrage all done and ready for their corporate PR people to respond to when they got to their desks at 9 am. They never stood a chance."

Fast-forward to 2019, and Walmart has learned its lesson well.

At a recent conference on 'Modern American Working Life', the company put itself at the forefront of understanding the problems Americans face in a rapidly changing world. Already America's largest private employer, Walmart unilaterally increased its 'minimum wage' to $11/hour – over a third above the federal minimum – and is now the US' largest provider of healthcare.

It has also carved out a role for being an important hub 'for' communities – especially small-town and rural – where many smaller retailers have been driven to the wall by the speed and cost-efficiency of online providers.

Contrast this with the spate of stories over working conditions at Amazon in the digital drive to ever-greater efficiency where 89% of their workforce say that they are 'exploited' and report gruelling conditions that might be comparable to a modern-day Victorian workhouse. None of this may be 'illegal', but rather like the company paying no federal taxes in the same year that it cleared over $11 billion in profits, it didn't take an ethics professor to tell that the whole thing stank to high heaven. Walmart wants to be different.

In 1984, a bright 18-year-old by the name of Doug McMillon started a summer job at Walmart unloading trucks at the distribution centre in Arkansas. It was the start of a lifelong career that has seen Doug work in different functions, and in 2014 he was appointed the CEO.

McMillon told us that his strategy was built upon some of the fundamentals of Walmart's original DNA, namely community, economic security and health and wellness.

These are not corporate 'buzzwords' to the company the Walton family founded in Bentonville, Arkansas. They go to the essentials of why Walmart was founded in the first place. To quote Doug, "What we see is that work is not just a pay check. For us, it is the foundation of a meaningful life. The sense of self-respect, personal growth, community and a shared purpose are fundamental to this."

In other words, there is something ineffably *human* about Walmart, something worth hanging on to in the dry, digital world of the online marketplace. McMillon believes that the retail differentiator for Walmart is through empathy. In other words, showing that they really do care and doing so in a way where their customers can feel it.

Led by in-depth research that shows that consumers do not only want the lowest prices possible, rather the 'best elements of click-to-order and bricks 'n' mortar', Doug McMillon is embarking on a radical revitalising of the business. As well as using the very latest (and impressive) artificial intelligence technology to map store layouts and staffing procedures, Walmart is training its associates specifically in demonstrating *empathy* and *caring* for customers. Whether through verbal communication, body language or myriad other ways, Walmart believes they can deliver that 'extra 10%' – while delineating clear, blue water from purely online competitors – by showing us simply that *they care*.

Walmart is far from alone. Although brands' emotional connectedness with their audience is nothing new, the primacy of it in the digital era is.

We seek out the local, tangible and tailored as never before. In a world where algorithms claim to know us better than our spouses, we covet the real, *human attention* that we have recognised since before we could speak. As McMillon says, "The only constant these days is change." But if Walmart's researched and rigorously thought-through strategy is even partly correct, it will mark a breakthrough in our understanding of the economics of emotion.

Threat or reward?

The American physiologist Walter Cannon introduced the 'fight or flight' response in his book *The Wisdom of the Body*, first published in 1932. In more recent times, Dr David Rock has popularised how leaders can become more effective by understanding human behaviour with the cognitive workings of our brain. His assertion is that modern social and societal 'threats' (such as online bullying) have precisely the same effect on our minds as the physical dangers and sabre-toothed tigers of prehistoric times.

Through his research, Rock has codified the five social domains in which we experience the threats (and rewards) which motivate our behaviour. He calls these the SCARF© model, and this is outlined below. The important thing to consider here is that the way we communicate sends strong signals to our audience of our intent and if they receive those messages negatively, then it is likely to invoke a fight, flight or freeze response.

Status: How we are seen in relation to others, our importance, influence and power within a community. **The communication angle: Am I saying something that will make you feel less important?**

Certainty: Our ability to predict (or influence) our future, for instance, through job or financial security. **The communication angle: Am I saying something that will create confusion or more ambiguity?**

Autonomy: The level of control we have over our own day-to-day lives and the things that happen to us. **The communication angle: Am I saying something that makes you feel that decisions are out of your hands?**

Relatedness: Our, almost animalistic, sense of security and 'safeness' among others – our 'tribe' or community. **The communications angle: Am I saying something that will make me feel not part of what you are planning or doing?**

Fairness: Perhaps the 'least animal' domain of our lives, our sense of fairness and justice between ourselves and other people. **The communications angle: Am I saying something that could be perceived as being unfair?**

Just consider how many times you have said something either in person or maybe via an email message, and the reaction you received wasn't quite what you expected. It is extraordinary the number of times we come across leaders saying, "I don't know what's happened, but the message received isn't the one that was intended."

Why does this happen? Often it is down to a lack of clarity of the message itself, but frequently it comes down to not fully considering the emotional needs of your audience and touching one or more of the five SCARF model domains.

This unintentional yet frequently authentic miscommunication will trigger what the author Daniel Goleman describes as an "amygdala hijack." Namely, the most primitive (or reptilian) part of your brain that is designed to ensure survival. When that happens, you will experience an emotional reaction that can include sadness, surprise, fear, anger, disgust and contempt.

We have found that a common Nimblicity characteristic of authentic leaders is their ability to quickly match their message to the mood of their audience. Some are able to do this instinctively, but others need to plan this more consciously.

The SCARF model is an excellent checklist for leaders looking to communicate and engage at an emotional level with their audience. We use it as part of the research when conducting the ORACLE test by asking what could be said that may trigger a SCARF reaction. Will the message set off alarm bells with your audience and push people away or put them into fight mode (think about most negotiations with union representatives here)? Or will the message make them feel good and, in turn, engage and bring people closer to you?

The reality is that in many cases, the former tends to apply.

PepsiCo and fuelling the selling machine

Of course, for every success we cite, there is an equal and opposite number of failures that we have worked on. Strangely, audiences seem to prefer hearing about these, for some entirely human reason…!

While working for PepsiCo in the mid-90s, the company was implementing a massive transformation programme of their Frito-Lay (snack food) business in Europe, the Middle East and Africa (EMEA). They called it 'FSM', Fuelling the Selling Machine, and the team had three key objectives:

- First, to guarantee that the overall strategic message was clear and understandable.

- Second, to ensure that information flowed freely between the various project workstreams.

- And lastly, to communicate with all employees on the milestones and progress we'd made on the programme.

It's fair to say that 'Fuelling the Selling Machine' hit the SCARF jackpot when it came to setting off unintentional amygdala hijacks. Describing it as a turn-off to employees would be an understatement.

For a start, people didn't want to work for simply 'a selling machine'. Yes, profitability is vital to any business… but so is what you are all about. The 'Why'. And so, through making everything about 'selling' and 'the bottom line', we'd holed ourselves beneath the waterline before we'd even switched on 'the machine' (let alone mixing up our metaphors to an almost manic degree).

That message put the business – profit – at its heart… yet it was really supposed to be about the employees. They were the ones we needed to deliver the change (i.e. increased sales) and yet, we'd excluded them altogether from the picture. And if these were the key strategic errors, tactically, it was – if anything – even worse.

For a start, it wasn't really clear what the company needed its people to do differently. Literally, what new behaviours did we need them to adopt? We'd failed to understand where employees were FIRST before we engaged with them. So as a result, when the message came through, it appeared to be confused, cluttered and utterly impersonal. Unsurprisingly, it was often forgotten almost as quickly as it was delivered.

Ultimately, Fuelling the Selling Machine led to the closure of the EMEA headquarters in the United Kingdom and the creation of a new regional headquarters organisation in Switzerland. We learned many painful lessons about 'cut-through', not least the importance of thoroughly listening to your audience's perceptions before you start – and putting them in the picture from the get-go.

And it also helped us understand that it's not just people who need to be authentic – it also applies to the message and the channels of communication you use as well. If these are perceived to be contrived, then your audience will disengage very quickly.

In the absence of smart research, it can take a rude awakening for companies and campaigns to understand that you may have an authenticity gap; namely, what they think of you is not the same as what you really are or what you were trying to SAY.

Authenticity builds connections during a crisis

There are moments when communication from leaders can turn adversity and high emotional stakes into opportunity, sometimes in the most unexpected and unorthodox of ways.

Following a period of spectacular post-war economic growth, the 1990s became known as the 'lost decade' in Japan as a result of continued economic turmoil and recession. Despite this, in 1997 Nike was investing heavily in Japan, with founder Phil Knight confirming at the opening of the Nike town store in New York that the first flagship international store would be in Tokyo.

However, by the beginning of 1998, the Asian financial crisis had cut into Nike's profit and battered its stock while an inventory glut had prompted the company to slash retail prices worldwide. Combine this with growing anger (and a boycott of their products) about labour practices in their factories; Nike was going through a tough time, and this resulted in an announcement to the NYSE to 'resize' the company by making 25% of the global workforce redundant.

Tough decisions needed to be made. At certain key moments of crisis, we need to hear from the leader. After all, that is what leadership is. It is why, when a shuttle explodes, it is the President that addresses the nation. If your Deepwater Horizon oil rig blows up, only the CEO will do when it comes to a public explanation (we'll let you judge whether that was well-handled or not). And in the current furore over social media publication of hate speech, bullying and terrorist propaganda, it was Mark Zuckerberg who appeared – on a booster cushion – to advocate Facebook's case before Congress in 2016.

The trouble was with Nike in 1998, nobody could find Phil Knight.

Having been the face of so many inspirational and motivational employee messages for the business during the good times, Nike's enigmatic, quietly spoken and surprisingly self-effacing founder had gone AWOL.

He was eventually tracked down to an Oregon mountain retreat and eventually persuaded by those closest to him, such as Nelson Farris, to rally the troops and do his 'CEO bit' at a town hall event at The Bo (named after the American baseball and football star Bo Jackson) sports hall in Nike's worldwide headquarters.

With a packed room of employees waiting to hear from Nike's spiritual leader, Phil emerged from the shadows and slowly walked to the podium, where he started by thanking everyone for coming along to the town hall and giving him the opportunity to talk about the challenges faced by the company.

He then went silent. And after what seemed like an eternity, Knight quietly spoke just a few words: "I really am so sorry. This was never part of the plan, and certainly not what I ever intended to happen." He couldn't go on and stumbled apologetically from the stage.

But instead of the reaction we might expect today, in our era of heightened rage and demands for 'heads to roll', the atmosphere in the room was quite the opposite. They felt empathy, compassion and humility for him, not the words which often get much play at the podiums of CEOs today. But Phil Knight had earned them. His employees felt them. Phil Knight was Nike's story, after all, and they felt like he was all their stories.

The *authenticity* of how Phil Knight felt and the fact that people connected with his emotion and he connected with theirs became a turning point for the company. Despite the pain of redundancy, Nike rallied, and the business rapidly moved on from strength to strength. Phil Knight's own reputation – already well-established by that point – was solidified as one of the genuinely 'good guys' of American business.

People sometimes asked later, "but surely people wanted to hear more from him – his plans to recover the business, and so forth?" The response is always the same. He showed more of himself in those three minutes of Nimblicity than any of his contemporaries would've done in a lifetime of slick corporate videos. For that audience, at that time, only total transparency and honesty would've done the trick. They knew him, and he showed that they could renew their trust in him and what they all had to do to succeed.

Authenticity trumps facts

"Hmm," the guy – steel-haired in overalls, a lifelong Democrat, with the tattoos to prove it – furrowed his thick brow. Until that point, our focus group in Green Bay, Wisconsin, had been running like fingertips on silk. But this felt like a key moment. Sometimes, a focus group moderator's most effective weapon is silence. Why was he – who had put his cross in the box for Obama twice, John Kerry and Hillary's husband the years before that – now seriously considering voting for Donald Trump?

While this was before his horrendous MTV leak, Trump was already well down on 'trust' among voters of all stripes, who cited everything from misnumbered Trump Tower floors through multiple affairs and Vietnam draft dodging.

"Oh, I get it. Trust me," he finally answered, after some prompting. "Trump's a bull shitter. I mean, he sells real estate in New York

City for a living… What do you expect?" Then his countenance darkened, and his eyes narrowed as he focused on his thought. "Yep. Trump's a bullshitter… but Hillary's a *LIAR*."

It is hard to think of a more lucid explanation for how America perceived the difference between two such (in the eyes of the rest of the world) diametrically opposed candidates in 2016. Overseas eyes may have looked aghast at Donald Trump, but, to many Americans, he spoke an *authentic* language they understood.

Understanding the new technology intuitively, he found a way to remove all the 'filters' modern audiences are so familiar with. He is exactly what he appears to be (and unashamed of it): self-obsessed to the point of flagrant narcissism… venal… uses money to keep score… utterly unapologetic. They still voted for him in their millions and, while he ended up losing, even more people did so again in 2020.

Why? Because such a brazen parade of character flaws convinced people that he was, in the end, authentic – and in that sense, being true about himself. In focus groups, we heard phrases such as, 'he's a business guy'… 'doesn't need to do this…' and, 'can't be "bought" – not in it for the money'. Aided by a façade of business savvy, courtesy of the wildly successful 'reality' show *The Apprentice*, Trump also understood the power of social media, Twitter especially. For the first time, pop stars or potential presidents could speak directly with their audience 'with no filter'. And Trump knew how to keep himself in their gaze with a constant stream of idiosyncratic, individual – but undoubtedly real – content.

In all the realms where communication counts (which is to say, all of them), authenticity – or the perception of it – has become the most salient of attributes. Few, if anybody, can really tell if Donald Trump is unhinged or the 'very stable genius' that he advertises. It doesn't matter; *what you appear to be is more important than what you are*. And this bit of timeless wisdom is as true today if you are a venture capitalist running a change management programme or Sophie Hinchliffe, the vlogging mum looking to pass on handy home cleaning hints. We have always prized what we perceive as real and human.

Authentic courage

How often do we divide our 'work' and 'home' selves? Or the public and private spheres, if you prefer? Yet, these distinctions are becoming increasingly blurred, both because we think we 'have a right to know' about those who lead and manage us and because we put more and more of our private selves into the public domain.

There may well be merit to this. The bestselling author Dr Brené Brown defines 'courage' – the Latin original – as meaning "the heart to tell your whole story." In other words, courage is essential to being both vulnerable and authentic (indeed, some psychologists now measure *vulnerability* and *courage* as precisely the same).

In Brown's words, real courage means the willingness to do something where there are no guarantees. It means the willingness to say, 'I love you' first. It means the will to put your hand up first. In short, it means the willingness to truly believe in something. And that will, literally, be the heart of your story. As an audience, we have developed a real appetite for this kind of 'courageous' storytelling.

When taking office at the age of 29, Alexandria Ocasio-Cortez became the youngest woman ever to serve in the United States Congress. As part of the opinion research testing her astonishingly successful insurgent ads, the most effective part of Ocasio-Cortez's campaign was the story she told as being 'one of us': a hard-working woman of colour against a privileged, rich, out-of-touch member of the elites (her Democrat opponent).

Since then, many people have questioned her authenticity as a member of the 'real' working class because of where she grew up or her access to funds. The point here is that this is really irrelevant; what counts is whether people *believed* it to be true of her. And they did.

While today the line between our public/private selves may be finer, it is unquestionably still there. Donald Trump's first presidential campaign was built on his persona as a 'successful businessman', but enough people believed that story to offset myriad other questions about his personal failings.

For Ocasio-Cortez, being seen as an underdog, working-class woman wasn't just a 'nice-to-have' to boost her 'favourability' rating; it was central to the story of her strategy.

A key strategic lesson flows from these examples. Back to our ORACLE test, the investment you make in your research will pay off handsomely when it comes to achieving your outcomes. Understanding the terrain upon which you are fighting and the story that voters are telling themselves are critical inputs into your strategy. The bottom line is that if your approach is discordant with the context they feel, you are unlikely to persuade them, no matter what you do. Finally, the person who lodges their story first in the minds of the audience – also known as 'framing the debate' – will win the debate.

Nation and cultural authenticity

Britain's last Labour prime pinister, Gordon Brown, could arguably be labelled a communications disaster while at Number 10. However, as a party elder and *former* prime minister, he came into his own as a voice of resonant reason. He persuasively argued for the Union in the successful 'No' campaign to Scottish independence, while his interventions for Remain were among the strongest in what was otherwise a lacklustre campaign. He has, perhaps, been most prescient in recently noting that "the tail of English nationalism is wagging the British bulldog." So, what does this mean?

Brown highlights the difference between authentic 'British nationalism', which is one of the most inclusive nationalisms conceivable, being open to Scots, Irish, Welsh and Celts equally – as well as more recent arrivals, everywhere from Somalia to South Africa.

This version of the UK's national identity has never been more under threat in the history of the Union. In 2019, almost two thirds of the Conservative party membership wanted to see Brexit 'delivered', even at the price of breaking up the union between Scotland and England. English nationalism – a more curious and monochrome repudiation of 'Britishness' – is on the rise.

Few embody this more completely, perhaps ironically, than New York-born Boris Johnson. During his terms as London mayor, his former advisor Sir Lynton Crosby was fond of pointing out that what was remarkable about our own blond Conservative bombshell was not his popularity. Rather, it was *his lack of un-popularity*. Whether it was being visibly able to laugh at himself on popular BBC TV shows such as *Have I Got News For You* or stuck halfway up a zip wire at the London Olympics in 2012, Boris appealed to a very English sense of not taking oneself 'too seriously'.

This is emphatically not the case in Scotland, where Johnson's 'unfavourability' rating nudges just over 60%, according to our recent data. The Scots simply don't appear to 'buy' Boris's personality in the same way as middle England, instead viewing him with a decidedly more European scepticism.

But in the realm of projecting 'authentic British charm', there could only ever be one winner. Boris and Brown came together, briefly, in support of London's winning those 2012 Olympic Games. Brown, as ever, stood, granite and gloomy, darkly suited, looking like he was preparing to administer the last rites to somebody. Without warning, Boris crashed onto the stage – and very nearly into the Prime Minister – waving a British flag while grinning broadly to his press-pack constituency. Brown never saw it coming... Boris has never looked back.

We are in the age of the 'reality/personality leader', which is another thing entirely from real leadership.

Microsoft – two leaders, two personalities

"Two nations divided by a common language" was how Sir Winston Churchill noted the gaping cultural chasm between the US and her 'mother country'. The 'mother tongue' had already been hopelessly abused and adulterated in the eyes of the greatest of British leaders. We shudder to think of what he would make of the cross-pollination now, as we pick up idiosyncrasies and idioms from boxsets and broadcasts, everywhere from Alabama to Australia.

Overseas readers will struggle to place, let alone pronounce, the town of 'Reading', where Microsoft has its British base. It is, perhaps, best known as the birthplace of the writer (and sometime stand-up comedian) Ricky Gervais, as well as the inspiration behind the hit TV series, *The Office*.

Back in 1998, Bill Gates's fortune had just hit the $50 billion mark, and, in a similar way to his contemporary Phil Knight at Nike, he had a revered status of being the spiritual leader of the global technology revolution amongst the 400 employees at Microsoft's UK office. The prospect of a two-day trip to meet royalty, prime ministers and employees was greeted with the kind of excitement that normally happens when the Pope visits Ireland.

At the last minute, Bill changed the schedule, and rather than doing an all-employee town hall, he said that he would come along to the annual All-Employee Family Day, a sort-of forerunner to 'bring your kids to work day'. Either out of his (undoubted) genius or, perhaps, astonishing luck, he asked to meet and be interviewed by the kids themselves.

The children weren't intimidated by the world's richest man. In fact, they asked straightforward 'kid questions' in that simple way that adults find so difficult and employees would never ask in fear of looking stupid in front of the boss.

> *"What's it like being the richest man in the world?"*
>
> *"Who's your favourite inventor or hero?"*
>
> *"What do you do with your days off?"*
>
> *"What's the most expensive thing that you own?"*

It would've been incredibly easy for the billionaire to come off as political or patronising, but he didn't in the slightest. He answered each one on the same level as it was asked, and his slightly gawky, scruffy, nerdy appearance only helped him to communicate with these kids. His authenticity shone through in a way it simply never would've done had he adopted the 'standard', pre-scripted, beautifully lit, stage-managed corporate PR event. The effect was priceless.

Although it bypassed those who were there at the time, it was also undoubtedly somewhat deliberate. What the display communicated to the British workforce was that he was more like them than perhaps they realised. Like many of them, he was a software engineer at heart (albeit 'chief software architect'). He'd obviously discovered his passion when he was young, and he'd stuck with it. As so many of them had. There was none of the grandiose grandstanding that people perhaps would have expected of someone who consistently topped the Forbes 'Rich List' for the two decades from 1995. He was, actually, ordinary. Comfortable in his own skin, whether chatting to a five or 50-year-old. And it made him even more impressive as a result.

Gates still has that understated charm, as any cursory YouTube surfer will be able to check out for themselves. It makes a stark contrast with that of his former 'number two', Steve Ballmer, who also visited the United Kingdom frequently during this period of the late 1990s. And it's important to recognise that, while there is no 'right' or 'wrong' in conveying authenticity – we all have our own individual and idiosyncratic style – it is fair to say that Ballmer's first visit didn't quite strike the same chord as Gates'.

Ballmer's performances have become legendary (and, thanks to the internet, widely shared), but in *The Office*-era Reading, it would be fair to say that other than those who had been to several global Microsoft 'WSM' (Worldwide Sales and Marketing) mega-meetings in Las Vegas, the majority had no idea what was coming on the stage of a local school hall (at the time Microsoft didn't have a big enough meeting space in the UK for an all-employee event).

After glugging a bottle of water down, Ballmer sprang onto the stage like a bald, rutting silverback gorilla in heat. His face contorted into a Maori 'haka' expression, he jumped around the stage that had been set up for him like a WWF super villain (albeit one in serious danger of giving himself a severe stroke). He glowered, he bounced; his veins throbbed until finally he stood before the mic and bellowed, "I have got FOUR words for you British guys: I! Love! This! COMPANY!"

It would be fair to say that the sales teams absolutely loved the over-the-top display. They depend on passion for the product to do their jobs, and this guy clearly had it by the bucketful. The only trouble was just 10% of his audience were salespeople. The rest of them sat in stunned silence, and the conversation afterwards was more about the ridiculousness of Ballmer's performance as opposed to his message.

The lessons learned were multiple; firstly, that this kind of authenticity – even Steve Ballmer's – is a valuable commodity. But only in the right setting. You have to consider your audience, as every good politician knows. Boris Johnson's upper-class chatter has them rolling in the aisles at Tory party conferences; his register is altogether different if he is conducting a live phone-in on London Broadcasting Co. (LBC) radio.

Without first thinking about who you are addressing, your authentic enthusiasm can appear hopelessly misplaced. A bit like throwing your granny into the middle of a wrestling ring.

True communications masters have learned to adapt their authenticity to a broad church. They firstly know their 'true selves' and are comfortable in that 'voice', but they also recognise how important it is to consider your audience first. You can switch people off quicker than a dull game of snooker without understanding their worldview first. For instance, Gates knew that – as for 99% of parents – their kids being treated well would matter more than meeting 'the boss'. And without needing to say a word, he communicated that authentically through his actions. Ballmer – on the other paw – managed to alienate 90% of his crowd before he'd even completed his first screamed sentence. He did give us all an almighty laugh, however…

Being funny… really

The late Australian broadcaster Clive James said that common sense and wit were the same things moving at different speeds; wit "is just common sense, dancing." And this is why we innately trust those we find witty. Laughter, after all, is involuntary assent. The danger for many in corporate and political life is that they don't realise how rare true wit is, with often calamitous results. And yet, we still invariably strive to be thought of as witty or 'funny' because the prize is so great.

There are myriad reasons to despise the Hollywood actor Ryan Reynolds. Apart from being voted sexiest man alive in 2010, he is genuinely funny and well-adjusted. He's built a brand around it. So, it is only natural to feel a slight tinge of jealousy and resentment when he used the action movie *Deadpool* to showcase his unique brand of self-deprecating humour. In his own words, he didn't want to create another action movie where the hero "spends most of his time staring into the middle distance, clenching his jaw muscles and squinting." He wanted something authentic that would also be very funny.

Whether or not you like the product is not really the point. *Deadpool*'s critical and commercial success is derived, in enormous part, from the sense that Deadpool is really Ryan Reynolds (further reinforced by Reynolds' hilarious and politically incorrect Twitter account). His personal brand is apart from a thousand other muscled male 'himbos', who look pretty but are capable of very little else... and he's used this to diversify into other businesses, from gin to football (he is now, somewhat bizarrely, co-owner of Wrexham Football Club).

Authentic wit is worth more than the output of a million 'creative department' consultancies. And it is far more effective. As with 'authentic' artisanal produce – whether craft gins or 'home made' furniture – we increasingly prize the authenticity of how these goods are sold to us. We don't want to 'feel' as if we're being sold to at all, in fact. So in order to be truly successful today, a sense of an authentic connection conversation – rather than a 'sales' conversation – is the balance you must strike. It's not always easy to get right.

The story of the princess and the janitor

There is an urban myth that the Queen thinks the whole world smells of fresh paint as everything is so clean and perfect when she visits anywhere. Anyone who has been involved in a royal visit will understand this, as the planning that goes into welcoming a member of the British royal family is designed to maximise every photo opportunity and minimise any risk of embarrassing moments.

In the late 1980s, British Airways had the honour of welcoming Diana, Princess of Wales to its base at London Heathrow. The red carpet was not laid out for the opening of a new terminal or for a flight on Concorde, but instead at the World Cargo Centre to see a multi-million-pound investment in new cargo technology. How 'the Queen of people's hearts' got roped into this was anyone's guess.

Nevertheless, Princess Diana glided through the assembled and completely awed neatly groomed managers. At one point, she stopped and chatted to a few of the cargo warehouse workers who had assembled in the areas designed by the PR folk to ensure that their proletarian presence was kept at a safe distance from any passing princesses. It is worth stressing that in the airline industry, these are the gruff, salt-of-the-Earth-types who spend their days lifting heavy cargo from aircraft onto the back of trucks.

Diana, by that point, well on the way to establishing her own independence from the royal household, decided to stop in her tracks and began talking to a chap who was known as 'Geordie'. Without wishing to appear indiscreet, it is only fair to note that Geordie was not known for his oratory refinement.

Diana had Geordie in her formidable gaze. From a distance, all you could see were two people who appeared to be sharing a hilarious joke. The sound of Diana's gentle cackle rose above the excited throng. At the same time, an increasingly audible panic emanated from the assembled managers, trying to move her on from this high-risk moment that hadn't been planned for. Whatever Diana's other faults and flaws may have been, she possessed a genuine talent for establishing immediate empathy and meeting her audience where they were. Aristotle would have applauded.

After they finished their conversation, Diana elegantly continued her journey around the warehouse, engaging in polite conversation with a handpicked audience. Nothing quite compared to the energy of the chat she had with Geordie.

Despite being asked, Geordie never did tell what caused the Princess such mirth, quite rightly keeping a small guard of privacy around a special moment. Rumour has it that she asked him what he had been doing today at work, and his reply was simply, "I cleaned up this shit hole before you arrived."

Nothing if not authentic.

And so, authentic wit – not necessarily the ability to be funny, but 'high-speed common sense' or 'abbreviated wisdom' – is a cornerstone of Nimblicity.

Together, we have worked with hundreds of leaders, and most do not have the overwhelming oratory skills of a Martin Luther King or Churchill. The mistake we often make is in thinking that we need to.

As we have found, time and time and time again, the ability to listen and converse with people from all walks of life is what stands out. And *empathetic* connection is what the masters of Twitter (including, to inevitable consternation, the 45th president of the

United States) 'get' instinctively: the person on the receiving end feels that he is talking to them personally.

This authenticity is priceless if you wish to *really* connect with Nimblicity.

LAW OF NIMBLICITY #8:

PRACTISE ACTIVE LISTENING WITH A GENUINELY OPEN MIND

"Most people do not listen with the intent to understand; they listen with the intent to reply."

Dr Stephen R. Covey

Couples' therapy lost a fine exponent when the former slave Epictetus decided to become a philosopher. He wrote, "We each have two ears and one mouth so that we can listen twice as much as we speak." He pointed out that the key to *any* successful relationship is an ability to truly set aside your own biases and beliefs… as well as the almost overwhelming urge to correct *immediately* what the other person has said. Instead we should take the time to *listen* and thus understand things from the other's perspective.

Whether in our professional or personal lives, it is not easy. And how often can we honestly say that we practise this, even in our most important relationships? And yet, this almost feline ability is as crucial to successful sales as it is to marriage. It is as vital as carrying a business with you through a period of change or winning an 'unwinnable' election.

This chapter looks at some of the underlying principles of why this is so… and how we can all open our minds and ears a little more to everyone's advantage.

A thought experiment...

Just for a moment, imagine your perfect Saturday afternoon.

Regardless of your usual routine or family commitments… what would it entail?

Where would it be – a windswept lake in verdant hills, perhaps, or a long, lazy sunny afternoon somewhere more exotic?

And how would you be spending your time? Actively or passively relaxed…? What flavours might be enveloping your senses? What images permeate your mind as, for 30 seconds or so, you just let it wander freely…?

In undertaking this little 'thought experiment' – apart from noticing how infrequently most of us actually let our minds wander for a little while – you also help illustrate the ways in which how we communicate is changing:

> **The picture in everyone's head is personal to them**. All great communicators make use of this: both the ability to use broad language to tap into something tangible and specific to you… and the primacy of the *visual*. A picture truly does speak a thousand words.

You might not know exactly what's in your 'ideal Saturday afternoon', but it's a fair wager that **you know exactly what it *feels* like**.

Listening will always be more potent than talking. 'Imagine a...' [it doesn't matter what]: A teacher you loved... A bully you despised... A time you felt perfectly content. Because of the emotional content, the *impact* is massively increased.

Asking a question immediately establishes a rapport between you and those you seek to motivate, move or connect with: 'Are you better off than you were four years ago?' 'Can't we do better than this?' or even, 'Will you come stand with me?' puts the audience firmly in the picture.

Some might call this the art of 'spin'. But wherever there is communication, there is 'spin'. After all, spin is simply the process of making your most effective possible case. And those with Nimblicity who will change the world in the 21st century – for good or ill – possess an acute sense of the emotional, which previously wasn't even much of a 'plus'. With the immediacy of the internet and the technological transformation it has wrought, it is a *prerequisite*.

Today, we reward a communicator's emotional intelligence over their straightforward moral rectitude. And being *seen to have listened* is a prerequisite for that.

The death of deference

As employees and voters, we are certainly far less deferential than in days gone by. Our tolerance for leaders who drone on for hours without considering that we might have better things to do is dramatically reduced. No bad thing, too. It is a dizzyingly short period since we took it on faith that our leaders were better educated than us, and better bred. In Britain, we believed they were of a better class too. No more.

Today, we certainly do not see our elected politicians as 'above' us... if anything, they are several rungs below, and thus, expensively well-read Oxbridge graduates in cabinet drop their consonants and adopt Estuary vowels in an effort to demonstrate that they really are 'down with us' and that they 'get it'. This is not effective listening or understanding.

We have borne painful witness to this ourselves. Once, during the 2009–10 financial crisis, while working for HSBC, during an employee 'Q&A', the bank's CEO attempted to illustrate that he 'got' the belt-tightening that all ordinary people were going through. "I'm putting four kids through [private] school," he complained. "It's not easy – I can tell you that." The conference collectively grimaced and inhaled as if to ask as one, "WTF?"

Equally, we can remember one well-known CEO who we worked with who was asked by a rather brave employee at a town hall meeting whether he could justify his salary (that had been widely reported in the press at the time). His response was that if everyone worked as hard as he did, then they could also drive around in a Bentley! The silence after the response was deafening and told the observers everything they needed to know about what his audience was *really* thinking.

Good learning material

One of the first, most fundamental ways politics is changing is this: our ability to *listen and learn* from the voters, rather than command and control them, defines electoral success. Leadership involves having the humility to acknowledge that if voters say something is an issue, then it is beholden on you to understand why. Not judge the voters as somehow misguided, misanthropic or misogynist.

The same is true in business as well, where leaders are having to be far more active in the way they listen to their constituents (namely, their stakeholders). Many a chairman and CEO has been caught out by not listening to shareholder pressure that has, in turn, forced them to make a U-turn on things like executive remuneration.

The Anglo–Dutch conglomerate Unilever was a good example of this when, in 2020, it reversed a decision taken to move its corporate headquarters from London to Rotterdam after a revolt by British shareholders. Ironically, one of the largest shareholders was the Unilever Employee Pension Fund.

In politics, previously solid Labour and Social Democrat voters have deserted those parties in droves in recent years because they got sick of the scolding they got from their supposed superiors. Aspirant working- and-lower-middle class voters heard themselves described as "deplorables," "bogans" and "chavs" by elites. Perhaps shockingly, the same voters concluded that the problem wasn't with themselves, but perhaps more with those smug souls seeking their votes. So they turned to new populist voices who sounded like themselves… or even, to the horror of paternalistic liberals everywhere, the old Conservative parties.

People increasingly identify through their 'group' rather than individual self-interest. So, it makes sense to engage with them on that basis. Group self-identification can vary from 'military voters' to race or sexual preference. Note that populist movements attract plenty of minority support. We will have a mixed-race majority in the US by 2050 and in Britain by the end of the century. What sometimes gets lost by commentators is assuming that people turn to populism because of the appeal of racism, bigotry or misogyny. This isn't just wrong; it's grotesquely insulting to voters who rejected the same tired tropes from 'leaders' who had *stopped listening*.

If you keep losing to populists and find yourself (in so many words) blaming the voters… you are looking in the wrong direction.

The writer Claire Lehmann wrote about the trend after Australian Labour's 2019 defeat at the hands of Liberal Prime Minister Scott Morrison. Morrison's Liberals were hopelessly divided; having ditched *two* sitting prime ministers, they sat well behind in the polls.

Lehmann laid the blame for defeat at Labour's inability to *listen* to what its core voters were saying (Sir Keir Starmer might take note here):

> *"No centre-left party has adapted or listened to what voters are telling them. Indeed, they lack even the vocabulary to explain what such adaptation would entail – which is why the left's recent election losses, from Alberta to Adelaide, are blithely chalked up to voter xenophobia or ignorance. Until the left finds a way out of this endless loop of toxic pre-election posturing and post-election blaming, such supposedly 'shocking' results as Saturday's are going to remain a regular occurrence.*

> *"Taking stock of real voters' needs would require elites to exhibit empathic understanding – such as acknowledging that blue-collar workers have good reason to vote down parties whose policies destroy their jobs; or that legal immigrants might oppose opening up a nation's border to those arriving illegally... What ordinary people want most from their government is respect, dignity and hope for the future."[7]*

Good business leaders, too, should want an unvarnished, *authentic* dialogue with their organisations. They know they have nothing to fear – and everything to gain. Vodafone's Arun Sarin would make sure that, yes, he would do employee 'town hall meetings' and all the rest. But he'd go much further, making sure that he went – alone – to call centres... to graduate training... to the staff restaurants and where the engineers worked.

Why? Arun said that it's because, "I hear it straight from these people in a really honest, raw way. None of it is filtered."

He knew that well-intentioned corporate PR types would seek *to please him*, noting, "If I ask people around me to tell me what they are saying, I know that it's going to get filtered... and I know that what I'm hearing is not necessarily always what they want me to hear... and I end up hearing things that actually are not always true and real."

That is listening with a truly open mind.

> *"What I love about this is when I go out and talk to people, I get real ENERGY from talking to people, but that's not all... I also get real insight, in terms of what people are thinking and what's going on in every part of the business."*

This helps explain why Arun Sarin was such a remarkable leader of a vast and complex organism like Vodafone. He understood that it was something deeper than simply a business – it was a community. And he used that Nimblicity to dramatic effect, inspiring a whole team and leading his company to record earnings and success. He deserves his knighthood – as well as our ongoing respect and friendship – as one of the most effective and excellent communicators we have had the privilege to work alongside.

AC Milan's generous 'stepdad'

Was 2021 the year that Europe's football clubs finally stopped listening to their supporters altogether? In April, it certainly appeared that way. After a year in which 'the world game' found itself played in eerily quiet stadia around Europe, clubs found themselves losing millions – and the largest didn't like that one bit. For a decade or two now, fans have felt treated like an irrelevant, noisy nuisance, and for owners who surreptitiously agreed with that assessment, the 'European Super League' was the answer.

In essence, Europe's (self-selecting) top 12 clubs would 'break away' and thus have more chances to play one another without the prospect of bleak trips to Burnley on cold November evenings. Bigger clashes would mean colossal TV revenues… and, thus, far less (if any) reliance on the pesky, messy fans coming through the turnstiles. From a business point of view, the logic was solidly grounded, if grim.

However, the 'human factor' had been utterly discounted. Nobody had bothered to check with those upon whom the game ultimately depends – the fans. And thus followed one of the fastest and most farcical turnarounds in sport (and business) history.

Within 24 hours, demonstrations had broken out at Manchester United, City and Liverpool against the plans. Managers and players alike – alongside Boris Johnson (cheerfully acknowledging his own lack of passion for the game itself) – found themselves uniquely united in opposition to the obvious attempted creation of an anti-competitive monopoly. Eight out of ten British fans declared their strong opposition, and within just three days, all British entrants had withdrawn, and various chairmen and CEOs found themselves victims of their own remoteness from their grassroots.

Some clubs still try to listen. AC Milan find themselves today in foreign – and non-footballing – hands. Elliott Advisors never intended to own a football club. The discreet, data-nerdy fund managers from Fitzrovia in London merely loaned some €303 million to Li Yonghong, the brash Chinese mining billionaire who bought AC Milan in 2017.

The Milanese have something of a track record with colourful billionaire types, having once been the property of Silvio Berlusconi (who was occasionally known to fly in to give 'tactical advice' to his expensively assembled team).

In this case though, an obscure clause in that loan deal would see the *Rossoneri* (the 'Red & Blacks') become the property of

Elliott in the event that Li didn't maintain his repayments. This duly happened – in a blaze of bad-tempered publicity – barely a year after Li had assumed control. And so, the financial fund managers found themselves not only the new custodians of Italy's most successful – but badly underperforming – football teams, but also the club's crumbling home: the legendary San Siro Stadium, originally constructed in 1926.

It is a truism of campaigning that appeals to 'stop' things are far easier – and more effective – than campaigns to do or build things. So, in spite of Elliott's genuine plans for a 'new San Siro' on the site of the current Stadio Meazza – not to mention a commitment of some €800 million to build the thing – opposition quickly arose. Despite its age and decrepit facilities (most of the toilets still involved squatting over a hole in the ground), "demolishing would be an insult," opined one local newspaper. It is "La Scala of football," screamed another, while another said threateningly that the project "would be a great embarrassment to [Milan Mayor] Sala and the Democratic party." A regional referendum on the project was mooted before anyone had sketched a single drawing.

Our job was to head off this assault and find out what Milan's long-suffering fans really thought. Not being able to talk about potential plans or ideas, Elliott's savvy leadership merely wanted to avoid 'losing before the game had begun'.

We needed to know where the Milanese really were, most especially the fans. A slew of quick 'n' dirty online polls had been commissioned by various media organisations (who love them because they are cheap and tend to generate the type of wildly unrepresentative findings which make great tabloid 'click bait'). We needed to know what the *Rossoneri* REALLY thought, and felt, about their club, their community and their stadium. Was the idea of a 'new San Siro' truly a non-starter?

As one put it, "my most cherished childhood memories are of sitting on my father's shoulders watching that beloved team." And this truly touched a nerve with his fellow fan. People – especially Milanese – associate their football with their *families and friends*.

The joy and euphoria the *Rossoneri* told us about was directly linked in their minds with their most cherished associations: community... camaraderie... and children. These matter far more in their minds than free wifi, 'nightmare' parking conditions and/or 'artisanal' food and drink that would be offered by an archetypal modern 21st-century stadium.

And here's the rub: they felt that the San Siro at present is in no way a 'safe or secure' venue to bring their kids. "The Ultras [AC Milan's own brand of hooligans] are really violent," one dad-of-three told us.

"What happens if we end up, by accident, in the 'wrong' part of the stand? How can I risk putting my kids in that position?" Furthermore, the deep (and genuinely representative) quantitative work we did backed him up on bathrooms, car parks, food and facilities. In no way did the current San Siro match Milan fans' view of their status among Europe's elite.

The project is still slowly making its way to commencement, with far less powerful headwinds than only a few months before. By understanding the deep-rooted emotional wellspring of Milanese attachment to (one of) their local football clubs, the owners have given them cause to believe that their new home will be for *them*.

New facilities, food and online capabilities are fine by themselves but would not shift a single supporter in favour of the project. However, by putting these attributes in the context of a deeper, more meaningful *story* – with them and their families at its heart – the fans listened. This would not be some concrete, soulless shopping mall of an edifice, but a living, breathing (and sustainable) representation of the best days of its past... and its future generations.

'Difficult conversations' begin with listening

The world is beset with consultancies selling you 'communications strategies', 'narrative development' or – God help us all – 'key messaging' advice. Virtually all of this has been made redundant by the nature of the way we communicate today.

What we really need help with is the art of conversation... and, most especially, *difficult conversations*.

Social media has reduced us all back to kindergarten – "You're wrong!" "No, you are!" "Are so..." "Are too..." "Snowflake!" "Fascist!" If you have the misfortune to spend much time on Twitter, this is unlikely to be 'new news' to you.

We speak – and more crucially – listen to our own side, aided by algorithms and our own desire to see our own beliefs confirmed. In doing so, we lose sight of one of Socrates' most wise maxims; '*It is better to be corrected and learn than to seek to correct somebody else...*'

And yet, as professional campaigners and communicators, we have more to learn from our 'opponents' than we realise... and they are more willing to listen to *you* than you see. In the increasingly divided world in which we find ourselves, some of our biggest 'wins' today are coming from encouraging clients to talk to people in groups 'outside' their normal bases of support. Conservationists find an open door when they change their opening approach to conservatives, for instance. Gay rights activists did the same when they courted the same group. Sanders, Trump and Biden likewise focused upon a demographic – the old working class – that Hillary Clinton largely took for granted.

And in business, the boards of large FTSE 100 companies like Capita, First Direct and Sports Direct have in recent years appointed 'worker directors' in an effort to introduce a fresh perspective to decision-making and improve engagement with the workforce.

In all these instances, the most important first step in a genuine conversation is **listening**. The theme is vital to communicating effectively in the new era.

Here are some of the principles to remember when entering any potentially hostile dialogue:

Stage 1 – REALLY LISTEN

Perhaps most obvious and also most fundamental: are you prepared to really listen? This means doing it actively (and no, not practising 'active listening' so that the other person *thinks* you're listening – this is an altogether more glib skill)… really listen more than you speak. That is hard, especially when some of your core beliefs are being not just challenged… but threatened. Step one means being conscious that listening is your primary goal here, not to somehow 'win' a debate, argument or interaction.

Leading sports coaches – from Vince Lombardi to Sir Alex Ferguson – thought that this was crucial to stepping up from a very good football manager to becoming one of the greats. Not to get 'too close to the woods' or take every training session. Really paying attention does not mean watching every kick of the ball. Instead, see the bigger picture and what is REALLY going on with your team, your squad and your organisation. This is a real challenge for the obsessives who tend to succeed in any domain, but it is vital. Obama's campaign manager David Plouffe said much the same thing: there must always be time to take a step back and listen.

As a focus group moderator and executive coach, one of the first skills you learn is the power of silence. Giving your interlocutor the time to think and gather their thoughts is a sign of immense respect; the equivalent of handing them the mic. It shows that you're serious and interested in what they have to say. How often we pretend to listen for a while – composing our response in our minds as we go – before diving back in, either 'parallel talking' (i.e. "oh I know what you mean because something similar happened to me…") or plain old interrupting. Train yourself in being aware when you do this.

As a practical step, repeating your partner's words back to them is an excellent technique, again much-used by (good) focus group moderators and executive coaches the world over. Good listening means getting what the other person actually said… not what you understood their meaning to be.[8] Getting them to be as plain-spoken as possible about how they reached their position, the logic they used to get there. And just as important as beginning the right way, know when to END a conversation. If there's a 'natural' end point, or perhaps you are both reconsidering your positions slightly (the sign of any good conversation)… then jump on that. Nobody likes to be bored.

Stage 2 – HAVE AN OPEN MIND

It is worth repeating: don't assume a posture of 'debate', but be conversational. We have lost count of the number of 'internally moderated' focus groups where a representative from Head Office will listen to complaints or criticisms of an organisation… before taking them each head-on and one by one. Infuriating for an audience. Remember that 'behaviour breeds behaviour', in the words of the Victorian matron. If you assume a 'learning' posture, your interlocutor will also. And the chances greatly increase that you will both learn from the exchange.

When you're in 'listening mode' (which you should aim to be at least 50% of the time – few of us get there, but it's a noble aim), ask epistemological questions.

Epistemology is the study of knowledge and beliefs. In other words, ask questions about their beliefs, not who they are as people. For instance, you'd be far better off asking, "what specific measures would you like to see taken on immigration, and why?" than, "does being anti-immigration make you a bigot, or did you hate foreigners and the poor all your life?"

We can all be judged on aspects of our work, appearance, family or family history. We instinctively rail against it because these don't say anything about our values or knowledge. Equally, we all lack a lot of knowledge – often about those very subjects we enjoy sounding off about. Admitting this simple truth is a fantastic conversation technique – "You know what? I'm actually not really sure about that..." Equally, asking somebody to illustrate their own epistemology. With the earlier example, asking, "can you explain to me how the immigration system actually works at present? What happens to someone, in detail, when they ask to migrate here?" is a far better way of understanding someone's position than assuming something from how they appear to think.

> *"Remember, you can be right or married... but not both."*
> – Anon, att. to Mrs Briggs

None of us actually wants to be corrected. It is a horribly human characteristic to mistake the thought that we could know something (such as vaccine success rates... the probability of the earth warming by 2° in the next 50 years... or our own abilities behind the wheel) before actually knowing it. This is so common that psychologists even have a name for it – 'The Unread Library Effect'. But even worse than realising that our own internal library remains, in fact, largely unread is having our views crushed by some smug loudmouth who hasn't really bothered to listen to us in the first place. You will have a much greater chance of winning someone over to your point of view if you have first made sure that you understand how their view is formed first… all the while being highly mindful of the fact that this apparent cretin may have something to teach you.

Stage 3 – EMBRACE OPINIONS ('Jedi Level Conversations')

By the 'advanced levels' of conversations, you will see, feel and know that taking some incoming fire from a bad-tempered Twitter troll is not a valid reason to throw yourself out of a window. You will become a *witness* to and observer of your thoughts as they arise… not merely their slave. As Thomas Jefferson said, "I never considered a difference of opinion in politics, religion or philosophy a cause for withdrawing from a friend." In only a tiny number of cases should a friend's position be so shocking or offensive to you that you simply must turn away from them. We must do more than 'accept' the other's point of view and their right to it. We should seek to learn from that right – and, to coin a phrase – defend it to the death.

Note how introducing new facts into an argument with somebody is usually the most ineffective way to persuade them to your cause. Except in very rare cases, this is more often than not likely to solidify them in their existing beliefs – especially when debating moral, spiritual and political questions.

This seems utterly irrational, so why is this? We human beings don't tend to construct our beliefs from a purely – or even majority – factual basis. We work the other way around, tending to believe or think (or, more accurately, feel) something to be true, then hunt around for facts and examples that back our case. When someone else produces a purely factual rebuttal to their case, it tends to cement them in their original view! This, which helps explain the 'Punch & Judy' back and forth of politicians talking past one another, is known as the 'Backfire Effect'. Being aware of it is critical to communication with those who do not instinctively agree with you.

We have explored the importance of shared values elsewhere, and these are critical to the most challenging of conversations. We can all develop a loathing for somebody close to us from time to time… but we share the prioritising of our children, and our home, and our dogs… and, hopefully, our relationships.

One useful technique to adopt comes from the world of improvisation comedy. Next time you find yourself slipping into a "No or yes, but" response, reframe it by saying "yes, and". The use of the word 'no' instantly creates a barrier, and 'but' signals that you are not interested in the other person's opinion at all. 'Yes' shows you are really listening, and the use of 'and' indicates that you want to build (and not dismantle) the other person's point of view.

Similarly, using a 'we/they' formulation has become a staple of politics, whether exemplified by, "We, the people"… or "We will be the ones who decide who comes into this country and the circumstances under which they come." With one word, you have enlisted an audience. Use your language to make your interlocutor a partner – not an adversary – and broaden the net of your appeal.

Conclusions… not confirmation bias

Getting out of the 'political mindset' is a good place to end this chapter – instead, to turn to the more *personal*, *tangible* and *local*. Ultimately, 'good listenership' is about demonstrating that you've heard – and possibly even prioritised – what matters to me more than you. And this is how you begin to understand how to change the world. Before understanding people's peccadillos, preferences at work or politics… understand their *beliefs*.

Remember that social media – for all its benefits and boons – has turned us all into broadcasters… it is not a great listening device. Trust your instincts and listen to those on the front line in your enterprise or electorate, especially those who will engage in the kind of constructive dialogues described above. Ultimately, these will tell you more than any 'big data' or polling exercise. *Paying attention to those around you* – the details and the discordances – will help you figure out where you truly want to go.

In today's rapidly changing world, we believe that leaders with Nimblicity are those who are able to *listen continuously with a truly open mind*. The sixth step of our ORACLE test is to evaluate by listening to your audience and adapt (again and again). Those who don't will quickly find that they are out of touch and out of time.

LAW OF NIMBLICITY #9:

BUILD COALITIONS TO ACHIEVE THE WIDEST POSSIBLE REACH

"People need to know what the plan of action is and how it will be implemented. Then they want the responsibility to help solve the problem and the authority to act on it themselves."

Howard Schultz, Starbucks

During the global rollout of vaccines for the COVID-19 pandemic, there have been a wave of celebrities from Pelé, Dolly Parton and even the Dalai Lama encouraging their followers to have 'the jab'. Many of us apparently prefer to believe Hollywood stars, Brazilian footballers and spiritual leaders on vaccinations over the combined, considered opinion of the Western medical community. But they merely serve as an illustration of *coalition-building* in order to reach as many followers as possible.

While some bonds have frayed – to the allegiances of class, trade and ideology which defined us a generation ago – new alliances have blossomed. We have argued in this book that new online forms of 'community' are no substitute for the real thing. But they offer valid and rapid access to whole swathes of potential customers, voters or followers with whom we previously would have had little contact.

The new communications landscape offers immense opportunities for those with the agility to interpret and integrate these new community bonds. We don't want to be led so much as advised, entreated and consulted. But our yearning for community is deep-rooted, whether that is for fellow gamers on the opposite side of the Pacific or other young mums who are struggling to cope.

The personal has never been more pertinent than in today's digitally connected world. In our ORACLE test, the leaders with Nimblicity are those who are able to leverage the plethora of opportunities for others to talk on your behalf and, in turn, have more influence.

A new approach to an old problem: Generation One

The plight of Australia's indigenes, or first peoples, is one of the most tragic and misunderstood, certainly anywhere in the Western world. In a country of 21 million (in 2008), 750,000 indigenous Australians led radically different lives in terms of life chances, education and longevity. Successive Australian governments demonstrated radically different approaches to the separation of 'black' and 'white' nations on the world's largest island.

In the 1990s, Prime Minister Paul Keating heard heckles and jeers turn to cheers when he delivered his famous 'Redfern' address. This legendary (in Australia) speech acknowledged for the first time the white settlers' "failure to bring much more than devastation and demoralisation to Aboriginal Australia continues to be our failure."

He then continued to its most famous passage,

> *"It was we who did the dispossessing. We took the traditional lands and smashed the traditional way of life. We brought the diseases. The alcohol. We committed the murders. We took the children from their mothers. We practised discrimination and exclusion. It was our ignorance and our prejudice. And our failure to imagine these things being done to us."*

In 2008, the then Prime Minister Kevin Rudd followed this up in the Parliament of Australia by making an official apology for the forced removals of Australian indigenous children (often referred to as the Stolen Generations) from their families by Australian governments. The impact of his words was huge, and they were understood to mark a beginning rather than an endpoint. Australians of all stripes wanted to heal the divide that so scarred their nation, but the question for Liberals and Labour folk alike was – how?

In 2008/09, mining magnate Andrew 'Twiggy' Forrest thought that he'd found the answer. Corralling an impressive group of media and advertising titans, including the Packer and Murdoch families, together in a room, he argued that this should be 'Generation One'; the moment where the 'gap' between black and white Australians began to close.

The first goal was an exercise in raising visibility — fortunately, a real gift of the new PM's — and awareness of the real issues. Unusually, the research revealed that the *facts* themselves should be pushed to the fore. They were emotive enough. Black Australians have a decade shorter life than their white cousins. Indigenous kids experience almost twice the rate of malnutrition and double the rates of suicide and self-harm as whites. Meanwhile, the employment rate was about half what it was for white Australia.

Such stark evidence of an almost (if accidental) apartheid-like divide in a 21st-century Western democracy (and at that time, by many measures, the world's wealthiest) stung many consciences.

Approval was gained to project handprints all over Sydney's iconic Opera House as a simple gesture of 'lending a hand' and getting involved. The effect was spectacular. The 'great and good' fell over themselves to be part of the movement that was being created to ensure that 'action' followed the words of the apology. Oscar winners Cate Blanchett, Russell Crowe and Kevin Rudd himself all showed up to the media launch. In terms of attention-grabbing, it didn't get much bigger Down Under.

Within the first nine months of the launch, the campaign had attracted some two million members to either offer support, sponsorship or genuine training possibilities for indigenous Australians. And despite Australia's seemingly permanently polarised politics, it was a truly bi partisan effort. The whole country seemed to want to help.

As a legacy of Generation One and our partners in the Australian Indigenous Mentoring Experience and many, many other organisations, the campaign persists to this day. 'Closing the Gap' reports are produced every year, while the problems remain stubbornly persistent. The latest points out that "the gap, in terms of life expectancy, is actually growing in 2020, not shrinking." Communications can only do so much.

The Constitution of Australia still does not recognise Australia's first inhabitants, and it may only be when the question of constitutional change (re)emerges that the issue regains its urgency. What price, then, for a renewed and reinforced effort to finally begin to heal the gaping wound that still bleeds from the very earliest white settlement in the land Down Under?

Climate of aspiration

There are few debates more likely to drive one to despair – and therefore more in need of hope – than that over climate change. While it can appear that there are some activists who actually want to see the planet boiled as a punishment for the evils of capitalism, there are still other voices that claim the whole thing is a 'hoax' and a waste of people's time to worry about.

The Amazon rainforests burn, even as the Brazilian President Jair Bolsonaro calls protections for the forests an "impediment to Brazil's right to development" and Western concerns about ecology and environmentalism examples of "imperialist" thinking. It can seem simply 'too hard' to think about a solution, especially as it is an issue that crosses national – and party – boundaries. The facts are well-established; surely the combined weight of our scientific, business and political leaders could come together to sort out a resolution?

Ted Halstead is the charismatic leader of the Climate Leadership Council (CLC), a unique bipartisan policy group, comprised of leading scientific experts (one founder was the legendary Professor Stephen Hawking), environmental groups (Conservation International and the World Wildlife Fund), industry representatives (including Allianz, BP and Microsoft), as well as heavyweight policymakers and economists from Washington DC.

The CLC's 'Carbon Dividend Plan' was devised by former Secretaries of State George Shultz and Jim Baker to bind both business and environmental groups uniquely into a 'grand bargain'. The idea was to come up with a proposal which could be genuinely actionable by the US Congress, balancing the need to curb carbon pollution with the genuine concerns of business.

Unfortunately for the vast majority of people, the language used in the world of climate change just doesn't resonate with the average person who now likes to consume information in 280 characters. Just as Joe Public wouldn't buy acetoxy benzoic acid for a headache, rebrand it aspirin, and you have a life-changing drug on your hands.

Our own research demonstrates that US public opinion has reached a 'tipping point' – most overwhelmingly in the under-40 age bracket – in the need to address climate change. However, what would be most critical to the CLC proposals' success was a strategic shift: they needed to engage with Republican audiences who have been all but forgotten by the liberal left voices who tend to dominate the climate debate. As the eminent LSE professor Eric Kaufmann remarked, "If Greta Thunberg wants to beat climate change by 2030, she needs to convince Conservatives and the middle-aged, not young, metropolitan liberals. This is possible only if environmentalism sheds its exclusive association with the liberal left."

And Kaufmann makes an important point. *If you are only communicating with those who already agree with you, you are largely wasting your time and money.* You only have to read the 'echo chamber' that exists in social media where people find like-minded souls and encounter what psychologists describe as 'truth bias', where we simply believe everything we see and hear.

As most Brexiteers will attest, no one challenges the opinions of Remainers in fear of a negative response.

For American Democrats – like their social-democratic European counterparts and Labour comrades elsewhere – the issue of climate change is self-evident. The planet is in crisis, and we must act. Beyond that, almost every other issue is secondary.

Meanwhile, the Conservatives were downright angry that "the other side of politics has got to monopolise this issue." These

Republican voters told us they felt 'overlooked', 'sceptical' and 'confused'. Make no mistake, they get climate change as an issue – but they question the veracity of the hysteria surrounding much of how it's communicated. Many could remember being told of the imminent risk of mass flooding 15 or 20 years ago, which didn't happen. Rather than more dire warnings, they wanted "the simple truth" and a "balanced approach" for dealing with the issue. Shrill voices increased their scepticism without answering it.

Specifically, they wanted to hear a more *hopeful* economic argument for climate action. Republicans are far more supportive of measures that were couched in American leadership, energy independence and regulatory efficiency.

The results of the research and deep analysis led to a clear and concise communications strategy to 'frame' the carbon dividends solution in 'Republican-friendly' messaging and a tailored language for talking about the proposals to myriad different audiences across the political spectrum that needed to be engaged.

Trusting people to say and do the right thing

In the 90s, the sports giant Nike became the subject of a coordinated campaign as a result of an exposé by the activist Jeff Ballinger over the working conditions in the company's factories and production plants in Indonesia.

Although the labour practices issues had been around since the early 1970s, the heightened level of anti-Nike feeling in the 1990s was being fuelled by a committed and unified trade union operation in the US and Europe. Their aim, while undoubtedly motivated by the emotive language of 'sweatshops' and 'slave labour', was to destabilise the business and improve their negotiating position with the management. It was highly effective too.

In spite of a Herculean effort by the business to (as they saw it) 'correct the narrative', nothing they did worked. Many of Nike's loyal employees simply did not want to engage on the subject matter, in spite of massive resources being applied by some of the smartest minds in the business. Emails, videos, internal marketing campaigns and tailored letters were sent to staff, setting out the company's good intentions and (real) commitment to human rights. Even the chief storyteller Nelson Farris couldn't convince them.

Unfortunately, outside of the management team, their efforts fell on deaf ears. It simply didn't matter what they said: their own people believed the anti-Nike rhetoric coming from the media and protesters alike – and, of course, this was being reinforced in their inner circle of friends and family. The circle of trust had been broken. The fundamental emotional connection that we all need with our employer had evaporated. And combining this with the Asian financial crisis we talked about in Chapter 7, the effect on the bottom line was all too visible to the leaders of the business. Gallup calculated that a disengaged team can cost at least a third of your bottom line, and in our experience, that is a gross underestimate of the real effect.

As we shall see with similar campaigns we have conceived, working on the other side of the fence, many company public relations professionals will always struggle in the face of a righteous onslaught of activists and advocates. Getting your 'key messages' right and clicking 'send' is never going to be enough. For Nike, we knew that the solution would come from those they trusted most. Not even Phil Knight or their boss, but their own colleagues.

In the spirit of Nimblicity, our first move was, in fact, to co-opt some of the best tactics of the activists and NGOs themselves. We also knew from the EKINs the power that an internal group of storytellers can have on the organisation, and this led to the creation of a team of Nike 'Citizen Journalists'. These ordinary and, in some cases, relatively junior employees were empowered to go on a fully expensed road trip in South East Asia and see the situation in the factories for themselves.

They were given cameras, journals, microphones and time. But far more important than that, they were given the trust and power to go wherever they chose and report whatever they found. In so doing, they were visibly being treated not as an audience to be corralled, but a trusted and valued partner on an issue that had shot to the top of the agenda.

The effect was immediate. As soon as it became clear that this wasn't some consultancy-driven exercise to try to 'disappear' the problem, but a sincere attempt by the business to shine a light into uncomfortable corners, many more people became interested and got in touch and involved.

With a highly unionised workforce, Nike's largest European distribution centre in Laakdal, Belgium became a real focal point for employee anger regarding labour practices in South East Asia. Rather than use a traditional town hall presentation to make the case for Nike, the enigmatic local general manager, Jan van der Torre, encouraged his team of warehouse employees who had been visiting the factories to share their stories in their own way and not in a company way.

They proudly set up huge displays in the main atrium of the centre as well as the canteen and spent time talking with their colleagues and answering even the most uncomfortable questions with transparency and honesty. There was no attempt to suppress or sugar-coat their findings by Nike. The result was palpable and had a massive effect in repairing the trust that had so eroded over the years.

From Laakdal to the world headquarters in Oregon, Nike's people — it didn't matter whether they were a lawyer, a sales associate or a warehouse worker – wanted to see what was going on; the good, the bad and the murky. They talked and asked questions of the reporting teams. We had videos, pictures and proof points that demonstrated that while, yes, the business had some bad practices to put right, it was doing so and according to the principles of fairness and transparency they had publicly espoused. This was critical; Nike was making long-term, positive changes out of the public eye and driven from a set of *values*, which are ever more fundamental to winning in the modern age of communication.

For Nike, the result was one of the steepest inclines in the level of employee trust and engagement we had seen in the company's history. It had entrusted and empowered its own people to speak on its behalf, just as the most effective political and charitable campaigns across the world do.

From being arch antagonists, employees became the strongest protagonists of Nike's commitment to be a socially responsible company.

It recognised that the 'old ways of top-down communication' were not working, and instead, it had to take a leaf out of its own brand mantra of empowering people to 'Just Do It'. Instead of seeking to impose command and control, it empowered its own people to tell the truth and, in so doing, tell a completely different story about the organisation they thought they all knew already.

In short, by engaging the right employees, Nike showed the power of Nimblicity in action by quickly embracing the collective strength of communities and people who could multiply their messages with influence across the entire organisation. Imagine the impact if they had done the same exercise today in a digital, data-driven world.

Those employees would have had a 'multiplier effect' by being able to amplify the message not just to their colleagues but to other decision-makers and influencers outside of the organisation as well as customers in every corner of the globe.

The digital multipliers

Today, Instagram 'influencers' are huge business, with PR promoters and branding deals to match those done by the biggest celebrities of the past. Influencers with up to one million followers can get $10,000 per post. For those with one million followers and up, they can charge $100,000 or more. At the very top, some achieve $250,000 for a single post or picture. Their daily existence, experiences and expertise – whether piano playing or simply cleaning the house – are logged on Instagram and YouTube to millions of fascinated eyeballs. And it is this very *authenticity* that the public is buying. It is precisely because Instagrammers appear friendly and familiar, the editing isn't perfect and the 'feel' is relatable. In short, it's because we feel they are more like us than any millionaire celebrity 'brand'.

As we have seen, our sense of trust in what we see and hear, and in one another, has been battered in recent years. This is why we find what is small, local and tangible to be beautiful. In our research all over the Western world, we find that people rarely trust institutions or individuals further afield than our hometown or district. Instead, we have created the age of the big 'me'. Personalised, individualised, our private lives made public property.

In 1988, we would've sought a little thrill from taking a look inside the *lifestyles of the rich and famous*. Today, we take pictures of our food – and our own lifestyles – and get a 'hit' from posting them all over the world.

Perhaps the biggest casualty of this era has been journalism, whether print or televisual. After all, the very meaning of the word 'media' means 'in the middle of'. We don't want to feel as if our lives have been 'mediated' at all. Authenticity and 'reality' make us all journalists now. But in so doing, have we replaced thoughtfulness in what we consume? The influencers and Insta-stars who stand out are those who have first done the work to know themselves and what they have to offer.

This is no accident. 'Brands' describe precisely what these people have become. And thus, the paradox; one of the biggest challenges for the industry as a whole is how to maintain that prized individual authenticity, even as blog producers and podcasters become million-dollar enterprises.

In the highly connected digital world we live in today, communicators and campaigners can learn a lot from the world of the influencers, especially in how they experiment, innovate and inspire their followers into powerful communities. The medium may have changed, but the message would be recognisable to a Greek studying in Plato's Academy.

Take the time to know yourself, create a vision that is true to your authentic virtues and vices, *then take others on a journey with you.* The future will belong to those who do.

Coalitions of community

In place of the old loyalties – perhaps to a company job-for-life or the hometown you never leave – today, we wrap ourselves in a bewildering web of community and 'tribal' loyalties. Many of these have the same unwritten rules and unspoken myths and memories as the old tribes we once emerged from. And they leave us with much the same age-old anxieties as we have always had: one variation or another on 'do I belong?'

As one gay friend recently put it upon coming out and attending 'LGBTQI' events as an 'out' person, she found her inner monologue incessantly demanding, "but am I 'Queer' enough?" Which, she laughingly remembered, "is just about the gayest thing you can ask!"

But is there really any such thing as 'the gay community', 'black community' or 'South East Asian community', in that there is as much diversity within each of those populations as in the rest of the human race? You might as well talk about 'the brown-eyed community' for all the use it is in differentiating us. Of course, the answer is 'yes' – there is a community wherever we feel a shared consciousness. But be warned, our 'tribal' loyalties are often not as strong as perhaps some of our 'community leaders' would wish them to be, and we find more powerful motivators.

For example, white women ended up voting for Donald Trump over Hillary Clinton, by 11 percentage points, in spite of Trump's recorded use of revolting, sexist language, which many pundits predicted would cost him the female vote. Similarly, Trump's Hispanic vote total of 29% in 2016 was two points higher than Mitt Romney's 2012 total, despite hostility to Mexican immigration being among the central hallmarks of his presidential campaign.

While, during the Brexit vote of the same year, voters' affiliation to their party 'tribes' proved not to be as deep as loyalty to a specific definition of British 'sovereignty'. In the end, the most effective predictor of the 'Brexit/Remain' votes was not political allegiance, region or race, but age.

Whether you are seeking political office or aiming to effect business change, successful campaigns are those that engage coalitions of different communities. Pockets of support for a strategy, cause or party may well come from sources that aren't immediately obvious to you. And this applies whether your campaign or change is global, national, statewide or local.

For instance, one prime ministerial candidate we worked for was warned that the business community, by and large, would "never support a Labour guy." Nevertheless, he went to small business forums and local chambers of commerce where he not only ended up picking up significant business support for his campaign, he also found that he learned a great deal about a subject many of his advisers were clueless about.

Bruce Notley-Smith was New South Wales' first openly gay MP whose campaign we helped to manage in 2011. Running for election in Sydney's prosperous and achingly liberal eastern suburbs, Bruce was contesting a seat held by the Labour party for 46 years. Nobody gave him a chance. While the party's central machine was pumping out the usual sterile messages about 'jobs and stopping the boats', this communication was doing little to speak to the local concerns of Notley-Smith's electorate.

So Notley-Smith went out and built coalitions with the local small business community, the environmental community and, in a first for his Conservative coalition, the local gay community. The result? He won over those who said that they could "never bring themselves" to vote for a conservative. Notley-Smith romped home and – four years later, perhaps more impressively – retained the seat.

Virtual communities of influence

It is almost lost to history that Steve Bannon, Donald Trump's campaign manager and for a while his chief strategist, started as a banker before becoming fascinated by the political potential of the ten-million-strong World of Warcraft online community.

Most likely at the other end of the ideological spectrum, the vegan community has grown exponentially in recent years, linking animal lovers with ecologists, as well as those looking to improve their heart health and triathlon times. Waterstones now stocks some 2,058 vegan titles in its bookstores, while over 600,000 Brits refer to themselves as 'vegan'; many more are vegetarian. Regardless of your opinion on those who hold these beliefs, for those interested in moving public opinion, this community is simply too powerful to ignore.

Doubtless, you will be able to think of many, many more web-based 'communities' depending on whatever fascinates you. Sofar Sounds is a start up that bills itself as "a global movement to bring the magic back to live music," while CaféMom is a community of "moms and soon-to-be moms" and WAYN does the same job, "helping discover where to go and meet like-minded people." But clearly, we are starting to use the term so loosely as to lose sight of its real meaning – and potency.

More loosely still, even businesses such as Airbnb, Uber and BrewDog (highlighted earlier) ascribe the 'community' label to themselves, which some excitable types have even sought to define as examples of a wholly new era of power.

The stories we tell as leaders, candidates and change-makers have a direct impact on the groups we seek to lead and influence. Our 'private' selves cannot be divorced – as perhaps in the past we could be – from the stories of our business, our campaign or our party.

In the same way that Steve Bannon recognised that the World of Warcraft community had mainly "white males with monster power" and that this could become a framework for building a political movement, the American academic Jonathan Haidt advises at least four steps to build communities that are most likely to leave a mark:

1. **Call attention to the traits people have in common, not what sets them apart:** Reach across the superficial divisions of race, gender and religion, and talk the language of shared values.

2. **Exploit Synchrony:** Have people move, play, campaign and work together in harmony. Neuroscience has shown that people are measurably more content when they move (or recite or sing) as a group.

3. **Create healthy competition between groups, not individuals:** People will always give more – and sacrifice more – for their colleagues and friends than some big abstraction (whether a company, slogan or union).

4. **Orientate your community around a shared moral cause:** Don't talk about employees or voters as a resource to be exploited, but as partners in a much bigger mission. Remember always the importance of why.

FOUR STEPS TO BUILD COMMUNITIES:

DO THIS	NOT THIS
Call attention to traits that people have in common	Find traits that make them different & set them apart
Exploit synchrony where people are connected	Use a 'divide & conquer' approach to connect
Create healthy competition between groups	Create competition between individuals
Orientate your community around shared moral cause	Make people a resource that can be exploited

And just like the hundreds of Nike employees who line up for the 'swoosh' to be tattooed onto their bodies, leaders and organisations should not be afraid of using symbols, rituals, flags and badges to bind communities of interest together. There are good reasons why those signs, symbols, myths and memories are so effective in binding us together as countries. They work on many different 'micro' levels as well. They allow a few simple themes or messages to be *amplified and grown through others*.

LAW OF NIMBLICITY #10:

MANAGE THE COMMUNICATION, DON'T TRY AND CONTROL IT

"Once you let the people in, they are going to want to do more. I know this violates everything they taught you at school, but you have to let go of the old style of business. Let the edges blur between customer and company."

Joe Trippi, *The Revolution Will Not Be Televised*

We tend to make four significant commitments in our lives: to a partner, to a vocation (not necessarily your job), to a faith (or belief system) and to a community. As with each of the four, our commitment to a community may not be something we overtly express — but there is something intrinsically human about our need to connect with others of a similar 'tribe'. And we feel it when it's not there. Yet, we still wall ourselves off in privacy — the more so, the higher we rise. It is astonishing, for instance, how many top politicians, executives and societal 'influencers' admit, privately, that they are desperately lonely.

"Happiness is only real when shared," wrote Christopher McCandless poignantly – his final written words before succumbing to self-administered poisoning, as famously told in *Into The Wild*. McCandless touches on something so profound and yet so simple that we risk missing it out altogether. Communication, like its siblings 'commitment' and 'community' depends, at root, on our *sharing* something – whether our thoughts, ideas and dreams… a common mission or purpose… Our very existence depends upon one other while our lives become increasingly enmeshed together.

Community is an acknowledgement of our interdependence – that our happiness doesn't just come from ourselves; it depends on others. And those 'others' are less amenable to direction and deference than ever before – as we have seen already. Thus, ceding control to others isn't just effective; it is essential to running a winning company or campaign.

Becoming a community-centric leader

The first principle must be to listen and *learn* from our stakeholders, such as voters, customers or employees, rather than trying to control them. Leadership involves having the humility to acknowledge that if people say something is an issue, then it is beholden on you to understand why that view is sincerely held.

Second, we must not seek to repress skin-deep discussions but *engage* with them. Social and political commentators talk about the rising growth of populism around the world, and the attraction to voters is because of racism, bigotry or misogyny. This isn't just wrong; it's grotesquely insulting to voters who rejected the same tired tropes from 'leaders' grown unaccountable and unwilling to have difficult conversations. If you keep losing to populists and find yourself (in so many words) blaming the voters, then you are looking in the wrong direction.

Taking stock of real people's needs requires leaders to exhibit empathic understanding – such as acknowledging that blue-collar workers have good reason to protest against actions that would destroy blue-collar jobs.

Third, we should beware of making too-fast generalisations over what and who is in your community. Today's ordinary people are not seeking draconian or demagogic actions but solutions to the very real problems faced by themselves and their families – just as they always have, in fact. What has changed in an ever more interconnected digital world is that the alliances between and within communities can now come together faster than at any time in history. It will require real Nimblicity to ride that future wave.

And lastly, you should link the communities you wish to engage with to your *story* as a leader. This is not about a more active personal Instagram account. It's about your personal 'narrative' and how it fits into that of your organisation. This is not to say that leaders aren't entitled to some sort of private life. Of course they are, but the *personal is political* like never before. Lean into that. And remember, too, that when the Greeks originally coined the notion of a 'private' life, they didn't think of it in a positive light.

This is why the root of 'priv-' is the same as '*de-privation*' – when we withdraw from the public discussion of who we are and why we act as we do, we are *depriving* ourselves of the opportunity to share in something larger. And this is Nimblicity in action. An ancient principle, re-adapted to fit modern times.

You have a nature, but you are not a slave to it. If you *are* humble, *be* humble and show how that benefits your cause. You may be brash and bombastic (without prejudice to any past presidents), but your audience will not care if those characteristics are put to greater use. Audiences increasingly tolerate faults and flaws, especially if we have overcome them in the pursuit of a deeper meaning. We want to know about the battles you have fought; it matters less what you are, builder, baker or banker, than why you made the choices you did and what you overcame to get here. In other words, the essence of your personal story.

One of the most common 'push-backs' we receive is that leaders don't want to 'share' too much of themselves online. Alas, for those people, we are moving to a world in which, if you put yourself forward for a campaign or change programme, it is simply your job to make use of the plethora of free channels now available to connect with the multiple communities that will ultimately determine success or failure.

Instagram now reaches *billions*, with 90% of its user base under the age of 35. Meanwhile, Facebook's average user is now 48. Linking all these channels together and engaging different communities with a similar message to what your audience is seeing in the news creates an 'echo chamber' effect, meaning the overall effect is far greater than the sum of its parts. You cannot do it all by yourself, and we would never suggest that you try. Amplify and influence through others.

One of the most striking by-products of the democratisation of the internet is that 'leaders' now emerge from anywhere overnight. Whether #MeToo's originator Tarana Burke (who coined the term originally in 2006) or an obscure Toronto psychology professor called Jordan Peterson having a similarly galvanising effect among (mostly) young men. The change-makers of tomorrow work more through collaboration and community than the purity of power of the past.

Authenticity, truth-telling and an ability to keep the conversation going – not simply communicate once a month or a year and have done with it – matter more now. 'Engagement' no longer means an annual employee survey (at least, not if you want it to mean anything). People expect to be *empowered*, and if they are… it pays back in multiples. But community-building, while creating that sense of autonomy, is no easy feat – and there are probably more failures than successes (don't worry, we feature a few of our own below). Those that harness that power source will reap the reward of the greatest capital we possess – our people.

So if the tech giants struggle to control what ends up on their platform, it's fairly futile for any leader wanting to exert any control of their narrative on the 'Wild West' of social media. Equally, companies have found that putting in place policies and procedures to govern what employees say online about their brand is completely pointless and that they will find innovative ways to anonymously say what they want anyway.

The smart approach is to engage those that can speak loudest on your behalf and let them do it in a way that they know will stoke the interest of the right people.

From our experience, the best and most influential communication happens when you have the courage to let go and give other people a message to carry on your behalf. Rewind 2,021 years ago, and Christianity established just one model for doing this.

Me to the power of WE

This means enabling groups or communities *within* your organisation to collaborate with you and on your behalf. While the meaning of 'community' has changed beyond all recognition, examples of communities – and the feeling of community – surround us still. Think of the sensory overload that accompanies you to a football match or your rugby club. A parent–teacher association meeting or a get-together of a local community group when a contentious issue is up for debate. Beneath the sounds and noise, the inner anxieties and outer smiles, there is also that sense of the tribal – of coming together with a common purpose.

This is not just limited to the world of the corporate or campaign. Take this account of clubbing in pre-millennial London from the always excellent Zadie Smith:

> *"A rail-thin man with enormous eyes reached across a sea of sweaty bodies for my hand. He kept asking me the same thing over and over; 'You feeling it yet?' I was. My ridiculous heels were killing me. I was terrified that I might die, yet I felt simultaneously overwhelmed with delight that, 'Can I Kick It?' should happen to be playing at this precise moment in the history of the world, and was now morphing into 'Smells Like Teen Spirit'. I took the man's hand. The top of my head flew away. We danced and danced and danced. We gave ourselves up to joy."[9]*

Imagine if we could bring just a shred of that feeling – that sense of sheer *togetherness* – to our working lives. Research repeatedly illustrates people's sense of lost *community*. For instance, the median number of 'friends I could call in a crisis' in the United States was five 40 years ago. Today, it is *zero*. Nobody.

While the bigotry and boredom of the post-war years can be happily consigned to the scrap heap, there is a sense of being part of something far bigger than the individual that HAS been lost. And the 'virtual communities' promised by social media companies and 'smart' phones are a pale substitute.

The search for community presents you – a change-maker – with both threats and opportunities. Even in nature, our primary expression of community is family (which is why appeals to family and family values remain so potent)... but what about other types of community?

Large organisations are made up of hundreds of 'mini communities'. And through bringing people together into groups of 'people like me', you can offer them something more profound than happiness, with more purpose and substance than the individual by themselves. Communities are the necessary bedrock for *all* change to take place. And that's what this chapter is really about.

Using examples from the worlds of companies, campaigns and charitable causes, we will examine how the importance of 'community' has grown. We shall give some examples of where it has worked well – and not so well – in both the political and corporate spheres. This will lead to some lessons for leaders and change-makers in creating an authentic sense of community in the organisations they lead. But first, let's ask whether the world truly is 'flat'; and to what extent 'old' power has been replaced by the new...

'New Power'...?

Some have argued that 'New Power' has fundamentally rewritten not just power structures in the world but also our fundamental values. For instance, GetUp! founder Jeremy Heimans has posited that we are more collaborative and participatory than ever before. 'New Power' (i.e. sharing-based) businesses like Airbnb and Uber, in this view, embody a wholly new 'DIY' philosophy. Whether through taking rides in your driver's own car or shacking up in someone's open spare room, we are all *partners* now.

Whereas power was once centralised and hoarded... today the network is the thing. The growth of, variously, the 'gig' and 'sharing' economies certainly has smashed up some antiquated business models, from mid-range hoteliers to London black cabs. And along with the excitement at the possibilities, many of the new 'movements' and 'communities' (… 'businesses' are just so 'old power', after all) have attracted equal parts of controversy and vitriol.

It is central to the idea of Nimblicity that the way we use power has shifted. But it is surely too much to argue that the laws of the universe have been fundamentally rewritten. How much 'power' do Uber drivers really have, for instance? (Spoiler alert: we have researched them extensively, and let's just say that 'empowerment' was not a recurrent theme among them.) Similarly, how peer-driven do we think our political leaders are, truthfully?

And have the traditional gatekeepers really been stripped of their power… or have the media barons of the 1970s and 80s simply collaborated and combined with the 'new media' oligarchs of the 2000s? It seems important to draw a distinction between the ability to bring together a 'mass movement', such as Occupy Wall Street or GetUp! – undoubtedly easier now than ever before – and actually turn those numbers into meaningful, lasting change, which is as tough as ever.

Nevertheless, Heimans et al. are clearly on to something. The web has made power more diffuse – but this has not made us all wholesale advocates of connectedness and collectivity. Some communities have turned inwards instead.

It is simply too early to tell whether we have entirely remade the machinery of power in the 21st century, but if you are to bring people with you on a journey, it is not enough to simply dismiss their concerns… you must engage with them. Real communities are about a real conversation between equals, not an artificial 'click and move on' experience. And if that takes you to some uncomfortable places, then so much the better. Nothing worth having ever comes easily.

Collective, conscious competitiveness and the 'world's favourite airline'

No business was more affected by the 80s outburst of terror than British Airways. Great Britain's national flag-carrier, which was still emerging, blinkingly, into life as a fully privatised company. The reality was the management simply had no 'playbook' for dealing with the kind of threat posed by rogue international actors, state-sponsored terrorism and planes dropping out of the sky in front of petrified customers. Word went around the company; we were in trouble. Our costs were too high, and incoming business had collapsed. It wasn't too much to say that a state of panic had enveloped the company – and it wasn't at all clear that the leadership had a way out.

Working at British Airways in the 1980s was a bit like working in a microcosm of the time. BA – like Britain itself – was about to be dragged, kicking and whingeing, out of the sclerotic 1970s – into the modern globalised economy that we know today. It was hardly ready for it. The company was divided by union and sectoral allegiances. 'Loyalty to the brand' would've been a meaningless concept because people didn't think that such a thing existed. You were loyal to your family, your workmates and perhaps the town or city where you were from… or if you were 'political', your class. These were the hallmarks of community.

In Britain, at least, work was where you went to waste your life. In that sense, at least, we differed profoundly from our transatlantic cousins, who always found a more puritan meaning in what they did for a living – their work. Class structures in wider society were imitated within British Airways itself. The disconnect was ingrained – and not entirely helped by the company's long-standing company newspaper, printed and distributed to the workforce, via branded bins every Friday afternoon, *British Airways News*. It was commonly known by the unions and the more militant employees as 'Pravda'.

In sharp contrast, the unions had established themselves as such a trusted source of information. One of the author's first 'big' jobs in private industry was to look at ways in which the company could communicate change for BA's ground operations at Heathrow Airport. The experiences of trying to effectively out-influence the unions were key lessons that have prevailed throughout a 30-year career in communication. The key one? Being part of the community is central to exerting influence.

It didn't take a month of focus groups (probably about five minutes) to work out why the union had such power and influence with the workforce; they were there, working alongside them… listening and learning from their colleagues, night and day. Today, we often think of 'unions' as a cosy, private club who look after their own – and with good reason. But in the 1980s, they were who we all turned to when things got rough. And they listened. They had embedded themselves in the employee community. Compared to that, a slick company 'newssheet' was never going to stand a chance. When the union demanded a strike, or work-to-rule or whatever, people knew where their loyalty lay.

As a senior figure puts it:

> *"They had a union rep on every floor to make sure that whatever the union said was absolutely resonating with the people within the workforce. And so, no matter what the company tried to do… no matter how rational their argument would be, it just failed EVERY single time with the people they needed."*

A business without any functioning dialogue between management and employees – let alone a relationship that festered like an embittered couple at the divorce court – was never going to be able to survive the aviation industry crisis brought on by terrorism.

Fostering good communication and community was key to fixing the three big strategic errors that BA had made:

a. **The message reinforced the divide.** Rather than building on the bedrock of a shared community with the same goal – which, after all, is what a thriving enterprise is – company communication was still driven by a 'top-down' ethos, totally at odds with the mood of the time. While Thatcher (and, later, Blair) were preaching the gospel of 'personal responsibility', 'ownership' and 'a stakeholder society', British Airways still addressed its workforce like errant children. The first and most fundamental change was to instil a sense of community in EVERYTHING we did.

b. **The language actively switched people off.** One of the hallmarks of communities is the language they share – think of the terminology of a passion you have and the (quite natural) sense of kinship you have with someone else who 'knows the lingo'. Employees, especially in such a technical, tight-knit environment like British Airways, are no different. Shared language implies shared interests and shared values… instead, BA insisted on a kind of strangulated formality that many people referred to simply as 'corporate bollocks' (some of you stakeholders are perhaps familiar with similar mission statements and memoranda). This had to change.

c. **The channels were not trusted or authentic**. 'Pravda' itself had become emblematic of a command-and-control culture that had its roots in a military-style set-up which had had its day. Pilots were typically ex-military from the RAF, and even ground staff wore uniforms that had epaulettes to denote their rank and status in the organisation. The democratisation that preceded it was in full view (and this before the advent of the internet, remember). After all, if you are truly to treat people as members of a real community, then they quite reasonably expect their voices to be heard. And so, out went the corporate 'newssheet', and in came 'listening sessions', depth interviews and dozens of other innovations that saw British Airways begin a genuine conversation with its workforce for the first time.

The reaction of employees, especially when viewed from a vantage point 30 years hence, was extraordinary. We expected crippling union militancy. Strikes or – if not – the kind of glum acceptance of 'reality' that crushes morale and productivity. But we saw something completely different. Rather than adopting a 'them and us' mentality, the business witnessed a remarkable expression of collective effort.

Recognising the need to reduce costs in the short term, employees volunteered for sabbaticals of six or 12 months. Many more – from the most senior to the entry-levels in the business – reduced their hours, or their days from five to four or even three days per week. (In many ways, it resembled the cooperative effort of the German car manufacturers during the global financial crisis, where lay-offs were avoided, in stark contrast to those seen in the States.) As a direct consequence of this *collaboration*, the business survived and thrived.

Perhaps more incredible than the bald facts of the effect on the 'bottom line' was the intangible impact on morale and motivation, pride in the marque that persists to this day. British Airways' people felt a unique mixture of pride, patriotism and loyalty to the company. This resulted in them not resorting to self-interest but a kind of rallying around the flag in the face of a range of potent external threats. Group identity trumped sheer self-interest.

One of the most dramatic and visible examples of this approach in action was the brainchild of the man at the very top of the organisation, Colin Marshall. So effective was it that it later became standard practice all over the aviation industry. Marshall became known for his 'Saturday walk-arounds'. It would be first thing on a Saturday morning, weekend workers blearily making their way to check-in, still perhaps trying to get that first coffee pumping into their veins… and there would be the chief executive of the whole operation, behind the check-in desk, asking questions, smiling and pumping hands. It went to the core of Marshall's whole philosophy of management, which was to be as visible and available to the entire organisation as possible.

It might not sound much today, in the era of CEO-led 'webinars' and vlogging for colleagues, but in the early 90s, it was revolutionary – and, more importantly, marked the beginnings of an approach that has become commonplace. Marshall recognised the changing context; people were used to more autonomy in their lives, they weren't going to tolerate simply being ordered around by some remote, imperial figure in a smoked-glass office. If the business was going to be modernised, and compete with sleek, competitive non-former-public-owned utilities, then the whole culture would need to change. People need to want to come into work, and a huge part of that was building a sense of community around the place.

Marshall began physically bringing people together in a dedicated series of events called 'Putting People First'. They came in groups of hundreds at a time from all over the world. Part of this was, yes, to get them all speaking the same language, as Marshall himself put it:

> "*I was anxious to inculcate our principles into the minds of our frontline people – those who had direct contact with passengers, including people in customer-service jobs, check-in agents, flight attendants, pilots and reservations agents.*"

This was about the creation of a culture. The bringing together of British Airways' shared community. On a basic, primal level it was showing people that they were part of a huge TEAM. There wasn't anybody else – 'The world's favourite airline' was… THEM.

Marshall was laser-like in his purpose here, giving every level of employee direct access to and explanation of the strategy. As well as the ability to question the folk who'd dreamed it up. There would be no slideshow, and the tone of voice was far less 'top-down' than people had ever heard from BA. The whole accent was on the experiential and egalitarian. This had never been done in the days of government ownership – even today, how many government departments would open themselves up to that kind of transparency?

Ultimately, the benefits to British Airways didn't just last a year or two; they went on for decades. Although the 'key messages' from Marshall's events were pretty quickly forgotten, not one of our colleagues from that time who attended forgot how they were made to *feel*.

There was a palpable 'buzz' about the place, especially around the people who'd been to one already. By the end of the programme, over 40,000 BA employees had attended – and virtually all came back changed. They had a WHY. A cause. A shared ambition. No longer was British Airways a place you went to waste your life – it was a community. For some, it could be the vehicle by which they achieved their life's ambitions. And even for those who did not, a deeper sense of loyalty now existed; to their team, route or department… their tribe within the larger business.

It is striking that, when the company was privatised, fully 95% of employees took up their share offer. And Colin Marshall's respect and popularity among staff was phenomenal – in spite of being the leader responsible for tough decisions in streamlining the workforce to ready the business for life in a harsh, private sector environment.

The workforce could have fallen into the comforting embrace of unionism and strikes, but they did not. Because Marshall had demonstrated the trust in them to engage meaningfully about a strategy for the future and given people a reason – a shared purpose – he had made them partners, financially as well as emotionally. Rather than opposing interests and values, workers and management had become part of one unique community.

Alif Ailaan, 'the Malala campaign'

A generation later, 2012 saw us recruited by a coalition (including the British government) to help establish a lasting campaign for girls' education in Pakistan. It had only been weeks before the impassioned teenage education campaigner Malala Yousafzai had been machine-gunned at point-blank range. Her crime? To write a blog for the BBC talking about her life under constant threat from theocratic thugs. Malala had had the temerity to advocate for a proper comprehensive education for young Pakistanis – of the kind we all take for granted in Western countries. Perhaps naively, the British Department for International Development (DFID) saw an election approaching on the Pakistani horizon and, with it, perhaps, the chance for change.

Pakistan itself was at cross roads, somewhere between military and civilian government. After the assassination of the iconic Benazir Bhutto, her former husband became Prime Minister Zardari (un-affectionately known as 'Mister 10%' because of his regular 'cut' on juicy government contracts) and governed nominally, in civilian terms. But the army lurked constantly, quietly in the background. Nothing happened without their knowledge or approval. While the judiciary represented a strong third pillar that kept the whole show from caving in, without ever having the strength to rein in the uniforms with the guns. Facilitated by Pakistani writer, intellectual and all-round 'PR guru' Adeel Jafeeri, we knew that we faced a steep, steep learning curve in order to be able to contribute.

As always, we began by initiating our own research. We found much evidence of the expected suspicion of the West – including the widespread belief that 9/11 was 'an inside job'. And yet, fully 96% of the country was committed to the basic right of female education. This was not the repressive, patriarchal caricature of Islamophobic lore.

A more nuanced picture emerged. The importance of the female part of the traditional family was emphasised. If we wanted to see more girls in education, we'd have to understand the context they lived in today – not simply try to impose our own. Girls are often critical to the survival of their family units. Layabouts, these are certainly not. Similarly, too often, there weren't actually schools to go to. Teachers' salaries were often not paid, and so – more often than you would think possible – educators simply didn't show up.

Then we arrived on the streets of Islamabad. Although we had taken care to organise insurance and evacuation plans, there is nothing quite like arriving in a place like that at 4 am (this around the time of the Benghazi/'Day of Rage' riots). It dawned that nobody really knew exactly where we were. And then our primitive 'tuk-tuk' taxi broke down at the side of the lightless road from the airport, in the middle of nowhere. Our plane landed in the days when the Taliban remained a real threat to Western aviation (as they may well become again), so landings were always in the awful hours between 3 and 5 am and the aircraft was forced to 'corkscrew' down to Islamabad's airport, one small rocket away from the 'Federally Administered Tribal Areas' (FATA).

Nevertheless, British government funding meant that the campaign was pretty well-structured from the get-go. The real danger was not falling into the trap of too many 'aid' projects whose staff spent too much time talking to each other while trying to secure ever more funding. So, we decided to focus on the most effective leverage that we had: the forthcoming election.

Despite Pakistan's sometimes shaky democratic processes, we believed that the general election would be basically free from the intimidation and ballot-rigging we'd seen in places like Zimbabwe (and it was). So, we engaged local communities to start holding their politicians to account. We would ask those standing for office to publicly sign up to an education 'pledge'. And then hosted real-world training sessions so that ordinary Pakistanis knew how to ask questions at public events and ensure that those voted into office stuck to the promises they'd made. This was far from easy but easily the most important legacy that we left behind – not a snazzy 'campaign'... but the beginnings of a change in culture.

Aid and development policy is changing now to ensure locals – wherever possible – take the lead in owning their own futures. We were well aware of the insulting colonial 'white saviour' complex and had no wish to be part of it. Instead, our aim from the beginning was to leave as much of our intellectual property and know-how behind so the campaign could live and breathe without us. And over the following year or two, we did.

We wrote the strategy, drew up the campaign book – so people would know what to do with any situation; election, event or emergency – and designed campaign (insensitively named, in retrospect) 'boot camps'. These were probably the most interesting and inspiring of all, bringing advocates together from all over Pakistan so they'd know how to fight effectively for girls' education and make sure politicians kept their spending commitments.

There is now a network of several hundred of these trained campaigners. Alif Ailaan's graduates still fight effectively for the cause of education equality across Pakistan today because of that groundwork and, most of all, because a 14-year-old girl refused to be bullied at gunpoint by masked cowards.

A multiplicity of moods – Network Rail

This sense of community and collaboration matters to us humans, whether you are trying to effect change in Punjab or Pontypridd. For instance, we found a hidden and untapped resource of immense pride in the work we undertook for Network Rail, the operating company for Britain's privatised rail network, soon after returning from Pakistan.

Here, though, the incredible positivity was drawn from something quite unique: a sense of history and institutional expertise that those in the rail industry still felt (and feel) towards their employer, whether it's called British Rail, Railtrack or Network Rail. In stark contrast to public opinion around Britain's reorganised national rail network, Network Rail's people felt hugely positive about the business – fully 85% of staff felt favourably about it as an employer, and in the crucial 'recommend' benchmark (used by many 'best place to work' measures), 83% of them said that they would recommend Network Rail as a place to work.

The challenge, therefore, was to harness that positive reservoir of emotion and remove the 'blockers' that (especially) frontline staff felt were preventing them from doing their jobs to the best of their abilities. A spate of negative headlines led to management adopting a 'safety at all costs' approach and, worse, a damaging perception that the leadership didn't trust their people. They didn't have a clear line of sight to the company strategy. There was a sense that dialogue had broken down almost totally between those working the lines and London HQ.

The answer was a phased programme – targeted at 300 of Network Rail's senior managers, initially – which was, at first, simply to communicate strategy more completely and concisely. The underlying aim, though, was to get across the unmistakable message that not only do we trust you... we are listening to you. Your voice matters – and it WILL be heard. Words alone weren't enough, so we ensured people had an authentic means of contacting decision-makers if they didn't trust speaking in front of colleagues (or, for that matter, us).

> *"An organisation's ability to learn and translate that learning into action rapidly remains the ultimate competitive advantage."*

– Jack Welch, CEO and former golf caddie

Meanwhile, leading the re-election effort of a successful European government a few years later on, the Prime Minister's personal popularity – and, more critically, underlying sense of trust and integrity – became the inflection point of the campaign. Ultimately posing the question "who do you trust?" displayed the effectiveness of *asking* the voters what they think – rather than simply telling them. Linguistically putting the control in the hands of the electorate – as you might equally with your own team – inspires their enthusiasm and, in this case, was answered with a landslide victory of historic proportions.

Rebuilding community and lost connections

It is usually far more challenging to communicate in an environment that is at least somewhat hostile. And, sadly, it is far more usual. This trend only seems to have grown, in our experience, in the age of 'offence' and confected outrage we inhabit today.

Take the example of Thales, one Europe's leading engineering businesses, who engaged us six years ago. Internal communication had almost completely broken down, in spite of the company being right at the cutting edge of high-tech defence technology. When we were interviewing 'staff', that invariably meant rocket scientists – or their equivalents – people with multiple degrees and jobs with mind-bending levels of complexity. Their levels of engagement should have been off the charts, but instead, they referred to one office as 'The Temple of Doom'; we heard about 'broken promises' and 'dumb decisions', while the business' communication function itself was labelled useless. Nobody was laughing.

Nothing is more likely to reinforce scepticism than a plea to 'trust me'. You don't establish empathy – an emotive connection – by simply denying what your audience feels. So in this instance, we instituted a raft of confidence-building measures.

Using exactly the same approach as peacemakers between two hostile actors where trust has completely broken down, we zeroed in on the believable, tangible and specific measures that could act as building blocks towards a larger structure of trust: weekly 'sit-downs' with employees were re-instituted, along with other popular measures (e.g. a Christmas lunch) that had been thoughtlessly cancelled along the way. We restructured the management team's communications programme, which had been almost entirely numbers (i.e. bottom-line) focused, and instead encouraged the celebration of success that had been important to the business' growth – and helped refire the ambition of a smart, driven workforce. Slowly, steadily, the company's 'internal engagement' – and staff retention – numbers began to recover and climb once more.

This story might well be part of a broader war throughout our society. On one side are the forces that sow division, discord and isolation. On the other are all those forces in society that nurture attachment connection, community and solidarity... It is not between one group of good people and another group of bad people. The battle runs right down the middle of every human heart.

Most of us are the problem that we complain about... Real commitment to a community involves moving from 'I' stories to 'we' stories. We may be dramatising somewhat, but it is worth every leader taking note of the battle lines we describe here and how we take them into account.

What unites all these examples is the edge each of these companies or campaigns sought – and won – through emotional intelligence in communication. Far from the supposed era of 'big data' or 'Moneyball' tactics to get ahead, it was the *human* aspect and an acute understanding of audience mood that made the difference. While increasingly it is possible to evidence everything from profitability to productivity, some are demonstrating that the 'human touch' of collaboration and *cooperation* can give you a crucial winning edge.

The optimistic continent

In the West, however, we are perhaps at the very height of individualism. 'Narcissism' scores – the number of people in the US, UK and Europe who feel that 'I am a very important person' or 'someone should write a book about me' – are off the charts. And yet, so are our feelings of *dis*-connectedness. Loneliness has become epidemic, while suicide rates skyrocket (and teen suicides are up 70% in the last eight years alone). We have looked at the causes of this elsewhere, so let us turn to both the effects and antidotes to our ever more atomised lives and what lessons there might be for would-be leaders everywhere.

This atomisation is emphatically not the case in other parts of the world. We have had the immense good fortune to do a good deal of work in stunning Sub-Saharan Africa. And one of the things that strikes you in this part of the world is that to be born African is to be born aspirational. With some good reason, too, as it happens. Of the five fastest-growing economies in the world, four are African. The continent as a whole is the fastest-growing on Earth, expected to increase by an average of over 6% every year until 2024. And you do not need statistics to tell you this fact – when you work there, you can *feel* it. Men will call fellow women (of no relation) 'sister' as a sign of kinship and community, for instance – indigenous folk in Australia and New Zealand share the same trait.

We had the great privilege to assist the Movement for Democratic Change (MDC) in Zimbabwe. Our efforts to help rid that glorious country of the freedom-fighter-turned-totalitarian tyrant Robert Mugabe saw hundreds of the MDC's activists beaten up – one of the author's included – as the dictator clung to power. And yet, the people *never* lost their sense of hope. Whatever the depredations of those in high office, their sense of optimism was as deep-rooted as it was infectious. Eventually, Mugabe was forced out – by his own ZANU–PF party – but it remains to be seen whether the 'new Zimbabwe' of General Mnangagwa meets the aspirations that greeted his takeover.

We found that Southern Africans are positive and optimistic *despite* – not because of – their elected politicians. Even in democratic, stable South Africa, the 'corruption' ordinary people see (an incredible 75% of whom said it was an issue of concern) couldn't dent the hopeful mood. Fifty-five per cent of South Africans said proudly that "my overall quality of life has improved over the past five years," while even more – two thirds – said that they expected things to continue to get better in the coming years. But focus group probing showed that they felt this had little to do with those in charge, for whom there was little respect or admiration.

This trend is not unique to Africans, even if many of us in the 'West' perhaps need to rediscover it.

Walmart

All this came to mind when we were invited to test perceptions of an innovative new policy initiative from Walmart – still the largest retailer in the US and by a significant margin, many are surprised to learn. The associate delivery programme – now an established and successful part of Walmart's e-commerce fulfilment operation – was initially proposed as a way of helping their associates who wanted to earn a bit of extra money do so.

They know their communities better than any long-distance parcel-deliverer also, so the answer seemed to be a classic free-market 'win-win'. The programme was entirely voluntary and, indeed, massively over subscribed when it was introduced. But is that how people 'on the ground' saw it?

The dozens of suburban blue-collar workers we interviewed did not give us an easy ride. The sense of insecurity and incredulity they feel when presented with some new programme or 'opportunity' by 'a suit' is (understandably) palpable. Some of this research took place in perhaps the world's most sceptical city – New York – so we were ready for, and received, plenty of bruising questioning… But the upshot of all that back and forth was that associates were, quite noticeably, positive about the whole idea of the programme, calling it 'common sense', 'welcome' and 'a way to work towards a better 'work–life .' There were three critical words they needed to hear from (and see delivered by) the business: advancement, respect and control.

Tone of voice was critical. In the age of transparency, 'the truth' counts. And there is no room left for safely vetted, inhumane 'corporate comms'. To modern 'blue-collar ears', this is worse than being disingenuous… it communicates disrespect. As in many other ways, employees are ahead of their employers here. Quite rightly, they do not see themselves as 'inferior' in any way, so are acutely observant of anything that smacks of patronisation or 'PR speak'. Stay on the level; show due respect.

Lastly, and most importantly here, was the concept of control. In a world increasingly without borders, safety nets or even functioning rules and regulators… putting control in their hands linguistically and practically – is the most empowering thing you can do. They wanted to decide when and where they worked. They wanted to decide how many packages they'd deliver and to where. They wanted to have a sense of control about how much they earned and how. For instance, it made far more sense for one dad to take on extra delivery work while his children were at summer camp – then hand it over to someone else when he wanted 'quality family time' around the dinner table. Command and control is obsolete; giving away control is in.

Walmart putting their associates in control of their hours, how they work, how much they earn and when is an attractive combination of both the 'traditional' and 'gig' employment models. Encouraging them to control the dissemination of the message, too, represented another. A colleague or co-worker enthusing about and recommending a new company programme, we noted, is hundreds of times more effective than somebody from head office doing the same – or a passive noticeboard or advertisement. When they adjusted the programme to make it attractive enough for associates to take notice of, they were happy to sell it themselves. They were in control.

For communicators – whether you are an aspirant leader, artist or activist – the Nimblicity lesson here is *leverage*. It is only through ceding control to those in your 'online neighbourhood' and networks that you can truly get your message across. There is simply too much noise for people to pick out, and pay attention to, your solitary voice. But there will be many others out there like you and who share your goals. Use them. Leverage them. Meet up with them. You will find that you become far greater than the sum of your parts.

Blur the edges and cede control.

Communication is meaningless without community

Giving others control begins by *understanding* them and the aims you all share. In our inter connected world, it is striking that the best communicators in the world are the most acute listeners. An almost feline ability to detect the mood of your audience helps define great leadership. And we live in an age where everything is measured. So, there's no excuse for not being aware of what's happening 'on the pitch' or on the salesroom floor. The more that you are aware of what's going on around you – among your audiences and stakeholders – the smarter and nimbler your response will be.

The director of internal communications at Sky recalled the story of how he was challenged by Jeremy Darroch, the then CEO, to fundamentally change the way they communicate with their 30,000 people. He said that the problem, in the age of digital polarisation, was that "everyone has a voice, but no one gets heard." The irony of this is that as one of the world's leading media organisations, they have a wide range of highly sophisticated channels that they can draw on to connect with their own people. But the reality is that they are not alone.

So, to close this chapter, what are some of the ways leaders can demonstrate greater Nimblicity and do better when it comes to ceding control?

Firstly, through remembering that *communities remain the very bedrock of our society* – over which we have allowed too much rubbish to accumulate. It may no longer be the traditional 'community' of town or village, but our need to belong to something – a group, a village, a tribe – is hard-wired, deep in our DNA. The World Wide Web has broken down the physical borders of country, state and city as effectively as it connects us with like-minded folk all over the world.

Your community might be founded on the values of veganism… or 'Jeeping'… or 'taking back control'… or the genius of Pink Floyd. It doesn't matter; one of the most beautiful aspects of the web is that you can be instantly connected to a group of like-minded folks who share your passions. And this is transforming how you, as leaders, understand your audience. Where we once sliced and diced our audience by age, or income or geography… today, we are just as likely to do so by shared interests, group identity or life stage. The world look is evolving every day, and for all our individualism… the appeal to community is stronger.

Underlying some of the most powerful changes effected by communication through social media is the 'levelling' directness it provides. Whether it's the chief executive or President… your audience can see 'it's REALLY him!' Professional 'PR' types feel the need to annotate their texts and tweets as such because of the backlash that ensues if they don't. Conversely, the surges that genuine interactions cause in the data are truly revolutionary.

And this leads us on to our ORACLE test and a consistent running theme: continue to evaluate by keeping your eyes on the METRICS. While the principles outlined above work, as we have sought to demonstrate, they are meaningless if you do not measure, measure, measure.

Virtually all platforms now offer simple, virtually infinite stats on how your last communication went over… A/B testing… and moment-by-moment feedback on your speeches, webinars and other communications. There is simply no excuse now for not knowing whether your message is getting through – and if not, WHY not? Similarly, those parts of the message that are better delivered by others closer to the ground – define them; enable and empower your people to take responsibility for their dissemination.

And cede that which you cannot control.

AND FINALLY...

Having reminisced on what we have learned during the researching and writing of this book, it strikes us that the lessons reverberate far beyond our worlds of business and politics. We have stuck to the examples we are most familiar with, but digitalisation has made communication today a whole lot quicker, more interactive and easier than ever before. What follows are some of the conclusions and consequences that emerge from the previous chapters.

First, a disclaimer: nobody knows how the jobs market will operate in 2050. Or how family life, politics or the world will have changed. Distrust those who seek to tell you they have the secrets to how these things will unfold. The louder they shriek – as with those shrill, self-appointed voices in the media – the greater your scepticism should be. It *can* be proven that these people get it right about as often as dart-throwing monkeys. So, we will seek to avoid falling into the same trap here.

The businesses and campaigns that succeed will be those that SIMPLIFY with the greatest agility and nimbleness

We are beset by more information, bewildered by more communications noise than at any time in human history. So much so that the World Health Organisation suggested in February 2020 that the world was suffering from an 'info demic' regarding COVID-19. And this unprecedented (we had to get the most over used word of our time in this book) era has led our workplaces to become dominated by a multitude of mail and chat channels – from Slack to SMS via Zendesk and WhatsApp. This, in turn, has created what one psychologist calls "the hyperactive hive mind."

A dizzying array of channels disenfranchises some, even as they empower others. As we re-emerge from the hibernation of lockdowns, businesses will have to strip back and *simplify* to succeed in how they communicate. And this will depend, in turn, on an ability/willingness to trust your people with a measure of control. The benefits will accrue to the bravest and those demonstrating what we have called Nimblicity.

This revolution is still playing out...

We are riding the wave of the internet revolution; it has not yet broken on the shore. The next wave of technology is coming up fast. We are moving from the Age of the Microchip to that of the Molecule. Elon Musk's Neuralink brain implant is being tested in chimpanzees (currently able to play video games solely through the mind). Musk has long argued that the factors that slow down communication the most by far are our poor, obsolete fingers and thumbs.

Imagine that future Donald Trumps will be able to broadcast via thought patterns. And if you have found the deluge of Zoom calls tiresome in 2021, perhaps don't dwell too long on the horror (or potential, as some would like to suggest) of holographic meetings in the not-too-distant future. As when Johannes Gutenberg invented the printing press half a millennium ago and Alexander Graham Bell patented his telephone in 1876, neither could have foreseen the harvests of those seeds they had sown.

Digitisation will democratise communication further

The trend continued and accelerated, from the mass 'readership' of the printing press, through the mass aural and then visual consciousness of radio and then television. Today, there is comparatively much less need for the gatekeepers of old. The 'media' – literally meaning those 'in the middle' – has seen their influence decline and diminish as we are all made guardians of our own brand.

Of course, it is possible for individuals not to 'play ball' and refuse to participate in the social media universe. Indeed, some of its founders now argue that we must. But businesses, charities, campaigns and office-seekers no longer have that option. You must play on the ground where your audience lies. So being conversant with new channels of communication is not a 'nice-to-have'; it is a pre requisite to success.

But the consequences for the psychology of an audience are still poorly understood

It is easy to rant about the new narcissism of Generation Z (those born between 1997 and 2015) or the apparent mindless triviality of what preoccupies the average punter, but that is to misunderstand their milieu. Narcissus was not a parable about vanity but rather of self-consciousness. We have never been *more* aware of our own image; at the same time, we distrust the '*image-makers*' who have gone before. Instead, authenticity and empathy – emotional connectedness – are more prized than ever before.

As citizens… employees… voters, we crave this connectedness. We crave community. Living as we do in a world where the CEO, Senator or Prime Minister seems puny in the face of global trends and events and yet too remote to answer the challenges faced by your family or local community. The answer, as we have seen, is to bring your message closer to the local level – empowering others to deliver a message on your behalf.

Smart, agile communication – *Nimblicity* – is about knowing that you don't have to connect with everyone to create influence

Just as Paul Revere made his famous ride in 1775 to warn the colonies (a good percentage of whom were still loyal monarchists) that the 'British are coming', it's about knowing who you can rely on to pass the word on to others. Who shares your values? Whose interests are also served should you achieve your objective?

Smart communication with *Nimblicity* is listening to what is really on people's minds

To see modern communications technology and social media tools as channels for 'getting the message out' is to misunderstand their entire purpose. By shifting your focus from the global to the local, digital media becomes the best source of intelligence and understanding you could have. Technology provides the tools to listen to your people better. It's what you do with the insights you get from listening to then show that you have heard them.

Influence through authentic communication remains a profoundly human thing

We could all do a better job of communicating with each other. We remain a fundamentally social creature, whether we like to admit it or not. The early era of the dotcoms saw the 'rise of the nerds' cheered in gleeful pronouncements from Silicon Valley. The more recent effects of 'techlash' have seen just how important person-to-person communication still is. Technology today is the enabler of that connection – not its *raison d'être*. Therefore, we should always put the people dimension first – ultimately, real connectivity is key.

From Aristotle to Zuckerberg – they *all* knew that effectively connecting with other people is about putting your *audience* first

Use your words to paint a picture with the people you want to connect with at its centre. This is as important to making yourself a compelling dinner party companion as it was to the founder of Western thought, Socrates, known above all for his *dialogues*.

Your best chance to influence is still through conviction… real connection and conversation. So, be brief and concise at the same time as saying something striking and surprising that you *truly* believe. Your ideas and inspirations are among the few things you can truly call your own. In the end, message matters most.

When we communicate, we're happy to label our audiences – voters, customers, employees, leaders, shareholders, media, NGOs…. the list goes on. But too often, the segmentation – the personalisation – ends here, and the 'one-size-fits-all' approach dominates. Those with the willingness and ability to tailor their message – to match it to the moment – will be the most successful future communicators.

Lastly, yes, power has become more diffuse, BUT…

The world is 'flatter' than it has ever been – in the ability of a person anywhere to rise on their merits or gain instant fame/notoriety online. But this emphatically does not make it more *equal*. COVID-19 has only exacerbated the differences and divisions between society's 'have nots' and 'have yachts', with the latter having seen dramatic gains over the past year – while society's most 'essential workers' have struggled. Another legacy that will surely see its consequences unfold over the next couple of years.

For us, this only means that communication will become even more POWER-ful as a tool for you to deploy. Real and authentic; clear and precise; nimble and focused. Those who are able to master the lessons in this book will greatly INCREASE their ability – and their power in society – through their effectiveness at influencing and amplifying others.

And here's our closing thought. We are *all* activists now. In a world where people have so many ways to gravitate to people *just* like themselves, Nimblicity means adapting to the needs of people who are no longer just your audience.

They are your partners, and that too requires a whole different mindset and approach.

ABOUT THE AUTHORS

Darren Briggs

Darren is the founder of Flametree Communication, a specialist leadership and change communications consultancy that has transformed the way leaders communicate with their employees in over 20 countries around the world. He believes that most organisations over-complicate what and how they communicate with their employees.

As an accredited executive coach and well-known speaker for several international business schools, Darren has over 30 years' global experience working at Chief Executive and Board level on employee, leadership and change communications. His award-winning corporate career has included a variety of senior roles for British Airways, Microsoft, Nike, PepsiCo and Vodafone.

With three children of his own all starting their journey in working life, he is driven to influence the leaders of today to change the way they communicate so that their approach enhances the employee experience for tomorrow's generation. And as a School Governor, he is passionate about helping kids understand that the way they communicate is the key to unlocking their future.

Just as he did… eventually.

Nicholas Wright

Nick is a leading political strategist who has managed countless winning elections, as well as business and social issues campaigns. He found himself tied up at gunpoint while campaigning to rid Zimbabwe of Robert Mugabe. He helped to lead one of Iraq's first democratic elections and spent over a year in Islamabad while establishing a campaign for girls' education in Pakistan. More recently, he devised the winning strategy for New Zealand's 'End of Life Choice' referendum.

He co-founded Sentio Group after a successful career in London, Washington DC and Sydney. The company uses the latest data-driven campaigning tools to assist clients in Britain, Europe, Australia and around the globe. Sentio's analysis has been featured in *The Sydney Morning Herald, The Australian, The Telegraph* and on the BBC.

When not running focus groups or campaigns, Nick can be found in a classroom. He loves to mentor students and lectures at Sydney University and NYU's campus in Abu Dhabi. He has the profound misfortune to be a fan of Newcastle United.

BIBLIOGRAPHY

Aurelius, Marcus. *Meditations.* Pretorian Books, 2020.

Boghossian, Peter & Lindsay, James. *How to Have Impossible Conversations: A Very Practical Guide.* Da Capo Lifelong Books, 2019.

Brown, Brené. *Daring Greatly: How the Courage to Be Vulnerable Transforms the Way We Live, Love, Parent, and Lead.* Avery, 2015.

Cannon, Walter. *The Wisdom of the Body.* W.W. Norton & Co., 1963.

Ebbinghaus, Hermann. *Psychology: An Elementary Text-Book.* HardPress Publishing, 2013.

Hall, Edith. *Aristotle's Way: How Ancient Wisdom Can Change Your Life.* Penguin Books, 2020.

Greene, Robert. *48 Laws of Power.* Penguin Books, 2000.

Green, Joshua. *The Devil's Bargain.* Penguin Books, 2018.

Haidt, Jonathan. *The Righteous Mind: Why Good People Are Divided by Politics and Religion.* Vintage Books, 2013.

Heimans, Jeremy & Timms, Henry. *New Power: How Anyone Can Persuade, Mobilize, and Succeed in Our Chaotic, Connected Age.* Anchor, 2019.

Holiday, Ryan. *The Obstacle is the Way: The Ancient Art of Turning Adversity to Advantage.* Generic Books, 2015.

Luntz, Frank I. *Words That Work: It's Not What You Say… It's What People Hear.* Hachette Books, 2013.

Rock, David. *Quiet Leadership: Six Steps to Transforming Performance at Work.* Collins, 2007.

Singer, P.W. & Brooking, Emerson T. *LikeWar: The Weaponization of Social Media.* Eamon Dolan/Houghton Mifflin Harcourt, 2018.

Sky, Emma. *The Unravelling: High Hopes and Missed Opportunities in Iraq.* Public Affairs, 2016.

Smith, Zadie. *Swing Time.* New York: Penguin Press, 2016.

Trippi, Joe. *The Revolution Will Not Be Televised: Democracy, the Internet, and the Overthrow of Everything.* Harper PB, 2004.

Westen, Drew. *The Political Brain: The Role of Emotion in Deciding the Fate of the Nation.* Public Affairs, 2007.

Willink, Jocko & Babin, Leif. *Extreme Ownership: How U.S. Navy SEALs Lead and Win.* Generic Books, 2018.

Online References:

JRE podcast, "Episode 1221: Jonathan Haidt," last modified January 7, 2019, https://www.youtube.com/watch?v=CI6rX96oYnY&t=188s

Lehmann, Claire. "At Australian Ballot Boxes, the Left's Empathy Deficit Came Home to Roost." *Quillette.* May 20, 2019, https://quillette.com/2019/05/20/at-australian-ballot-boxes-the-lefts-empathy-deficit-came-home-to-roost/

Endnotes

1 Sentio research, December 2019.

2 The statistics are, gradually, improving, but – as of 2019 – 15% of school-age South Africans are not attending school, at enormous cost to human potential.

3 Sky, *The Unravelling*, 201.

4 … And, less successfully, Theresa May's loss of that same majority two years later.

5 This is where the name saboteur – and sabotage, etc. – came from. 'Sabots' were wooden shoes worn by peasants.

6 Interview on JRE podcast, 7th January 2019.

7 Claire Lehmann, "At Australian Ballot Boxes, the Left's Empathy Deficit Came Home to Roost," *Quillette*, May 20, 2019.

8 …. This was demonstrated by Newman's notorious *'so what you're really saying is'* interview with Professor Jordan Peterson, which went viral precisely because of this effect: https://www.youtube.com/watch?v=aMcjxSThD54

9 Smith, *Swing Time*, 111.

Printed in Great Britain
by Amazon

80680309R00133